Linguistics: A Very Short Introduction

'Matthews is refreshingly unpartisan, extremely insightful in detecting
the strengths and weaknesses of different theoretical positions,
respectful of intelligently argued positions which he happens to
disagree with, and a doughty foe of fads and mumbo jumbo. He
has great skill in conveying complex topics in a clear, unbiased,
down-to-earth way.'
Professor Martin Maiden, University of Oxford

VERY SHORT INTRODUCTIONS are for anyone wanting a stimulating and accessible way into a new subject. They are written by experts, and have been translated into more than 45 different languages.

The series began in 1995, and now covers a wide variety of topics in every discipline. The VSI library now contains over 500 volumes—a Very Short Introduction to everything from Psychology and Philosophy of Science to American History and Relativity—and continues to grow in every subject area.

Titles in the series include the following:

P. H. Matthews

LINGUISTICS

A Very Short Introduction

OXFORD
UNIVERSITY PRESS

OXFORD

UNIVERSITY PRESS

Great Clarendon Street, Oxford OX2 6DP

Oxford University Press is a department of the University of Oxford.
It furthers the University's objective of excellence in research, scholarship,
and education by publishing worldwide in

Oxford New York

Auckland Bangkok Buenos Aires Cape Town Chennai
Dar es Salaam Delhi Hong Kong Istanbul Karachi Kolkata
Kuala Lumpur Madrid Melbourne Mexico City Mumbai Nairobi
São Paulo Shanghai Taipei Tokyo Toronto

Oxford is a registered trade mark of Oxford University Press
in the UK and in certain other countries

Published in the United States
by Oxford University Press Inc., New York

British Library Cataloguing in Publication Data

Data available

Library of Congress Cataloging in Publication Data

Data available

ISBN : 978 0-19-280148-7

Impression: 25

Typeset by RefineCatch Ltd, Bungay, Suffolk

Printed and bound by
CPI Group (UK) Ltd, Croydon, CR0 4YY

Contents

Acknowledgements

It would be silly to pretend that one does not need advice and help in writing something like this. David Hawkins, Sarah Hawkins, David McMullen, Anna Morpurgo Davies, Francis Nolan, and Lucienne Schleich have all supplied it in one way or another, some going to great trouble. To them especially I am truly grateful.

List of illustrations

The publisher and the author apologize for any errors or omissions
in the above list. If contacted they will be pleased to rectify these at
the earliest opportunity.

List of maps

Chapter 1
The study of language

What is *linguistics*? It is defined in dictionaries as the academic study or, more simply, as a 'science' of language. Those who practise it are *linguists*, and the aim of this book is to give some feeling for what interests a wide variety of linguists, and for the nature of language itself. What do we mean, though, by applying the term 'science' in this field?

Human language is, of course, uniquely human. I say 'of course' since, as it stands, that is scarcely a profound statement. It does make clear, however, that in studying language we are starting, and cannot but start, as insiders. We are ourselves human beings, and all speak at least one language. We are therefore studying a central aspect of our own lives. This puts us in a privileged position, since we take for granted so much that outsiders would find out at best with difficulty. Being an insider, however, also has its problems.

Other scientists have studied the 'language', as we are tempted to call it, of other species. We know, for example, that many birds sing partly to establish a territory; that honey bees tell others in their hive where sources of food are located; that the calls of at least some other primates are in part learned and not wholly 'instinctive'. Most autumns, when I am tidying up the garden, I am thrilled by the song of the European robin. It is the only garden bird that has an individual territory outside the breeding season, and therefore sings when others are silent. Its song is complex and can be divided into phrases, lasting on average between one and two seconds. Each phrase is different from the next, and can be analysed into 'motifs', which themselves vary. To that extent, then, we are able to see structure in the robin's song. Yet we have no evidence, as human scientists, that these smaller units have what we would call specific 'meanings'.

The autumn is also a time when professors must sing for their living. While preparing my lectures, I have often wondered what a similar outsider might make of the noises *Homo sapiens* so volubly produces. Let us imagine that some genuine aliens come here in their UFO to study us. Forget the conventions in films: they will not be able to question us in fluent American English. But suppose – though this is already some supposing – that they communicate with one another at a range of sound frequencies similar to ours, so they will at least hear what we are saying. They will find that, when we are together, we are rarely silent. Sometimes we give tongue while doing things that seem to have some purpose. We might at the same time, for example, be cooking dinner and then eating it. At other times we chatter, for long periods, while apparently doing nothing else that matters. We may be simply sitting down, moving limbs from time to time or shifting our position. There are even occasions when whole groups of people sit there while one individual spouts at them. This happens, for example, when a professor lectures to an audience of students. Our alien scientists might not understand at once that this is communication. Think how long it took our own intelligent species finally to grasp the point of bird song! Let us assume, however, that they have this insight. How would they analyse the sounds they recorded?

To us, as insiders, it seems obvious that speech includes words. If someone asks, for example, for three oranges, the word *three* is one word with one meaning, and *oranges* another with another meaning. But an outsider would have no easy clue to the existence of these words. Try, if in doubt, to listen to someone speaking a language totally unknown to you. There will be pauses when they breathe or hesitate, but no audible divisions among smaller units. Therefore, even though we take for granted that such units must be there, we cannot guess reliably where they begin and end. If that is not already convincing, look at the display in Fig. 1 overleaf, of a recording of three successive words as spoken naturally in English. The variations in the signal largely correspond to our distinctions between vowels and consonants. But it is not cut off between words. It seems then that an alien investigator might at first hear no more than an intermittent burble. How can they discover whether parts of it have separate functions?

The natural method is to try to correlate repeated signals with the other things that people are observed to do. That is how we can ourselves identify, for instance, an 'alarm call' in another species. Once this call is sounded by one individual, others in earshot can be seen to hide, or dash up trees, or fly off, or start running. But a moment's thought makes clear that language would only rarely lend itself to study in that way.

Take, for example, a group of people who are talking while they are having coffee. One of them has the coffee pot in hand and asks if anyone would like some more. We cannot, however, predict exactly what they will say. It might be 'Would anyone like some more coffee?', or 'Would anyone like another cup?', or 'Another cup, anyone?' In response to these and other possibilities, some individuals may hold out a cup and have it refilled; others at most shake their heads. In saying any of these things the speaker need not actually hold the pot. It might indeed be empty and, if anyone wants more, someone must go to the kitchen to refill it. If no one wants more nothing happens that, to an alien observer, will give any clue at all. Even when there is coffee in view and being handled, the word *coffee* does not have to be spoken. Neither is it spoken only when that is the case. A speaker might ask someone if, for example, they have remembered to put coffee on their shopping list. These are everyday exchanges. Where, then, would an alien find the

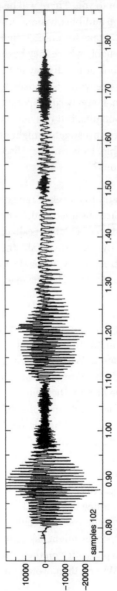

1. Wave form of *those three oranges*. This shows the amplitude of the acoustic signal, as it varies in time (left to right). The time dimension is marked arbitrarily in tenths of a second.

correlations that would demonstrate that speech is made up of such words, or that *coffee* is one of them?

It would be still more difficult if they were to look in on a course of lectures. The lecturer will be doing almost all the talking. When anyone else speaks it will be the lecturer who is usually addressed, not other members of the audience. Most of the time, students are engaged in making marks on paper. What sense would this make, if one did not already understand it? It might well be seen as powerful confirmation that, in general, human burbling did not carry detailed 'meanings'. Lectures might be explained as periodic rituals in which certain members of society, who are mostly older, assert dominance over groups of other members, who are mostly younger. This is not so very different from the robin seen by us as maintaining a territory. What we call sermons might be explained as part of a more complex 'dominance-ceremony'. Pop concerts might be another, in which lower-ranking individuals show subservience by dancing, cheering, and clapping. How close our alien observer might be to the truth, and yet how wrong!

The blessings of being an insider will by now be obvious. At the simplest level we already know, for instance, that some sounds are 'language' and others are not 'language'. (Imagine an outsider trying to work out the role of coughs and sneezes.) We know too that language is not uniform, that different forms of speech are found in neighbouring communities or neighbouring political units. Therefore linguistics must also be a science of, in the plural, languages. We know that speech is made up of specific smaller units, which are composed in turn of units such as vowels and consonants. We know too that there is more to language than just face-to-face communication about things immediately before us. Nor is it even necessarily communication. People think and calculate in language, trivially, all the time, as well as, on occasion, profoundly.

These are enormous advantages, if we try again to put ourselves in alien shoes. But the flip-side is that, as insiders, we must struggle hard to be objective. We too are talking men and women; and, for a start, we have no way of talking about language other than through language itself. Our 'metalanguage', as philosophers call a language in which one talks about a language, always has essential properties of its 'object language'. As human investigators we have no escape from this circle. I will try in this book to write 'we' when I refer to us as linguists. I will use other forms, like 'one', when I am talking about people as a subject of investigation. Any 'we' is nevertheless a 'one', and, in the last analysis, every 'one' is also a 'we'. Anyone who says, for example, that the word for 'bird' in French is *oiseau* is, like a linguist, using a language, English, to say something about a language.

A warning about meanings

Let us examine this statement about French more closely. I have written *oiseau* thus, in italics. This is the normal convention that linguists use in citing words and sequences of words, like *les oiseaux* 'the birds', or *J'ai vu les oiseaux* 'I saw the birds'. Another convention is to write translations in inverted commas: thus, for the word on its own, *oiseau* 'bird'. What then do we mean by talking of 'the word for "bird"'? The statement may at first seem quite straightforward. There are many kinds of creature in the world: birds, insects, snakes, and so on. People must be able to talk about them. Therefore any language has to have a word by which each one can be referred to. A word for birds has, we will say, the meaning 'bird'. In English it is *bird*, in French *oiseau*, in Spanish *pájaro*, and so on. But this leads directly to a fallacy, which is so fundamental that it was not until the 20th century that linguists and philosophers finally nailed it. When we talk about a language, we can do so, once more, only through the medium either of itself or of some other language. Our language has a word *bird*, with the meaning, as we say, 'bird'. It is therefore very easy to perceive this meaning as in some way prior to the word that corresponds to it.

The fallacy, in its crudest form, is that words are names for pre-existing categories. The following is a quotation from the Authorized Version of the Book of Genesis, in which Adam, who is still the only human being in the Garden of Eden, assigns names to other species with which he shares it.

> And out of the ground the Lord God formed every beast of the field, and every fowl of the air; and brought them unto Adam to see what he would call them: and whatsoever Adam called every living creature, that was the name thereof.
>
> Genesis 2.19

This is one passage that for many centuries lay at the centre of linguistic thought in Christian Europe. Another was the story later in the same book of the Tower of Babel. The naming by Adam explained the origin of language, as a way of labelling things around us. The second story explained why, as we know it, 'the whole earth' is not still 'of one language, and of one speech'. For, to curb mankind, God had to 'confound' it (11.1–9).

Now this 'confusion', whatever its origin, is certainly with us. There is, however, another way of talking about *bird* and *oiseau*. As words, both are in italics, and each word is used, *bird* in English and *oiseau* in French, in referring to a certain range of creatures. An English speaker might use an expression such as *those birds* to refer to various groups of them; a French speaker might use, of the same groups, an expression such as *ces oiseaux*. These are our basic findings, and they directly concern the way the words are used, first in one language and then in the other. But in presenting them we are again obliged to talk in English, or in French, or in some other human language. We therefore establish a convention by which the meaning of *oiseau* in French can be indicated by a word in English, in inverted commas, whose meaning in English is the closest to it. Thus, from an English viewpoint, we write *oiseau* 'bird' just as, from a French viewpoint, we might write *bird* 'oiseau'. We are not, however, appealing to a prior concept of 'bird', as a meaning that all

7

languages must have in common. The basic relation is again between the words *bird* and *oiseau*, between these and Spanish *pájaro*, and so on.

Once we see things in this light, we are less fazed when precisely common meanings do not exist. Anyone who learns French learns, for example, that no single French word corresponds to English *river*. *Fleuve* is sometimes used when *river* would be appropriate, but often *rivière* will be used instead. Nor, for that matter, do the limits of the use of *rivière* correspond quite to the differences in English between *river* and *stream*. Now French and English speakers have been neighbours for centuries, and their languages have much in common. Even in this illustration we can at least start from a rough correspondence. But in other cases an apparent similarity can easily mislead us.

Linguistics

What, for example, is the word for 'mother' in Navajo? Navajo (pronounced, as it is also written, '**Na**-va-ho') is the language of a people in the Southwest of the United States who have, so far, resisted being sucked into speaking only English. Their traditional culture is not, as we might anticipate, remotely like ours. Yet they too are born of women. We have in English a word, *mother*, that refers to this biological relationship between each person and their female parent. We might well think that, if any 'meaning' pre-exists by virtue of the world we live in, surely that does.

The anthropologists who first worked with this people found that there was indeed a form, *shimá*, by which they could translate English *mother*. But it does not follow that the use, or even a primary use, of *shimá* should be glossed as 'biological female parent'. According to a 1970s account by Gary Witherspoon, the whole cultural emphasis is on the affective action of a *shimá* in both giving and sustaining life. A *shimá* is a being who acts in that way; and, in a society intensely sensitive to the rights of other people and other creatures, every member of a mother's clan is, at one level, a *shimá*. So, at the first in a series of less general levels, is every

8

member who is female. The term is often qualified: for example, *shimá yázhi* can, though it does not always, translate *aunt*. Nor should we assume that a *shimá* is necessarily human. For it is not just people that give and sustain life. So, for example, does a cornfield or a flock of sheep; and each of these is a *shimá*. So does the earth itself, and the earth too is a *shimá*.

'Aha!', we say, 'but when one talks of "Mother Earth", one does not mean that the earth is literally a parent.' Certainly in English, where *mother* is used primarily in reference to a biological female parent, that expression can be seen as secondary. A dictionary will first give the primary definition; then a series of extended senses, in which the same word is applied to someone else who acts in part like a mother, to an object from which a run of other objects is reproduced, and so on. But, in the traditional culture of the Navajo, the earth is not perceived as merely 'like a *shimá*'. In Witherspoon's words, it is 'not only an actual mother but . . . also the greatest of all mothers'. For the earth itself is a living being who created the earliest Navajo people and continues to sustain her children. At this point we have barely scratched the surface of the cultural-cum-linguistic system in which *shimá* has its place. The example does, however, make clear that we cannot take a word in our own language and assume that there are forms in any other language that can be placed in simple correspondence with it. Still less can we take a word like *mother* and project from it a meaning 'mother', defined by other meanings such as 'female' and 'parent', which we assume that any language must distinguish from others. 'Meanings' are not simply given in nature, or in the way the world itself is. They are bound up with a culture of which language is one aspect.

The moral we draw is not just that one language can be strikingly different from another. We must also train ourselves to look objectively at what is said, in our own language or in our own culture, about language. The tradition that words are names has deep roots in our history, in Ancient Greece as in the Bible. It is therefore natural for us to think that, just as *Mary Smith* can be the name of someone who is visibly there, *bird* or *mother* or *love* are 'names' for what must, in some similar sense, be there. It is also natural to say what words mean in another language by putting words in our own language in inverted commas. When we say accordingly that *oiseau* 'means "bird"', we are tempted to think that a meaning 'bird' is something out there to which *oiseau* is related. We are tempted to say, by the same logic, that *bird* too 'means "bird"'.

Is that last statement strictly empty? I have not said that it is, and many colleagues would object if I did. It is harder, however, to be level-headed about meaning than it is in talking about words themselves, or smaller units such as vowels and consonants. Are these, at least, straightforward?

Words

That there are units like *bird* we can take for granted. We are, after all, not alien observers, but human beings whose investigation has more than a head start. But if we do not watch what we are saying, a head start can easily turn out to be a false one. The way I am now writing about language is, of course, in writing. It was therefore natural to identify such units by a word in writing: *bird, mother, oiseau.* It was indeed entirely harmless and it would have been silly to do otherwise. But what is harmless for one purpose can be prejudicial for others.

It is notorious that written English can be an appalling guide to forms as spoken. The *ome* of *come* does not rhyme with the *ome* of *home*; the vowel of *call* is like that of *haul*, where it is written *au*, *bought*, where it is written *ou* or *ough*, and so on. It will therefore be helpful at times to supplement the usual spelling with the kind of transcription often given, in square brackets, as a pronunciation guide in dictionaries. *Come* and *home* are thus, in the form of Southern British English represented in *The Shorter Oxford English*

Dictionary, [kʌm] and [həʊm] respectively: the [ə] and [ʊ] of [həʊm] indicate a vowel whose quality changes from beginning to end. *Call* is similarly [kɔːl], where [ː] is a standard indication that a vowel is long: compare the shorter vowels in [kʌm] (*come*) or in [kɒl] (*col*). Likewise, *haul* [hɔːl], *bought* [bɔːt]; also, in this form of English, *cork* [kɔːk] or *pour* [pɔː].

The letters conventionally placed in square brackets are those of the International Phonetic Alphabet (or IPA), designed for use in transcribing any language. A symbol like [ʌ] has accordingly an absolute value, to which the vowel in *come* is reasonably close. The IPA is nevertheless itself a system of writing and, unless we take care, it is easy to assume that each word, as it is usually written, can be transcribed separately. *She will come*, for example, is three words: *She*, or in IPA [ʃiː], plus *will* ([wɪl]), plus *come* ([kʌm]). In *She'll come*, the '*will*' is no more than an IPA [l] ('*ll*'): is this also three words?

An alternative is to see *She'll* as just one word: in IPA [ʃiːl]. Compare, for example, *feel* [fiːl]. The argument against this is that, as the apostrophe in the spelling indicates, '*ll* is a reduction of a fuller form *will*. But now take a word like *blackberry*. In writing it is clearly *black* plus *berry*, each of which is also written separately in, for example, *a black berry* ('berry which is black'). How come, then, that it is now one word and not two? The facts are that, as a separate word, *berry* carries relative stress on the first syllable. 'Berry which is black' is thus phonetically ['blak 'bɛrɪ]: the symbol for stress in the IPA, which now appears for the first time, is a vertical line ['] marking the transcription of both *black* and *ber-*. In *blackberry*, however, there is much more stress on *black*; and, in many forms of English, *ber-* then loses its [ɛ]. In place of it, there may be a vowel [ə] (called in the trade 'schwa'), which is often found in syllables without stress: in IPA ['blakbərɪ]. The [ə] is like the second vowel of, for example, *butter* ['bʌtə]. Alternatively, *ber-* has no vowel: ['blakbrɪ]. The argument then, in this case, is precisely that the '*berry*' is reduced. Even then, however, we do not spell things consistently. Why is *hot dog* not consistently *hotdog* (['hɒtdɒg]), or *monkey puzzle* not *monkeypuzzle*? Why should, for example, *boyfriend* (['bɔɪfrɛnd]) also be written *boy friend*?

Now imagine you are faced with a language no one has yet written. You find expressions that you know mean something like, in English, *She'll come, They arrived*, or *I'll have eaten*. How many words, then, are they? You cannot tell from their translations, since there are languages in which all these would correspond to single words, while, in English, the number varies. Such problems were often faced by European missionaries and administrators when they began to write the languages in, for example, southern Africa. Some tended, in practice, to be lumpers and others to be splitters, even when the languages were actually very similar. One problem, obviously, for linguists is to try and make explicit what 'words' are, and the criteria by which they are divided.

Linguistics as a 'science'

To study language 'scientifically' is, in part, to refuse to accept uncritically, or 'unscientifically', the ways of thinking that, ahead of any professional training, we all bring to it. We must strive to be as objective as we can, about individual languages and the nature of language in general. It is hard, but can be marvellously liberating.

'Science', however, is a word with many senses, and is often regarded as in opposition to what are called in universities 'arts' subjects or subjects in the 'humanities'. Our picture of a 'scientist' is quite likely of a man or woman working in a laboratory, with ever newer and more pricey instruments, who conducts experiments or develops mathematically sophisticated theories. A scientist's work then spins off into new technologies or inventions. Our stereotype of 'arts' subjects is of people working at their desks or in a library, synthesizing knowledge, exercising judgement, trying to develop insight. Before they leave school, many students who go on to university have already been directed into subjects on one side or the other. By the time they have taken their degrees, the other may be closed to them.

Linguistics straddles this institutional rift. It clearly has its 'arts' side, and its links with other subjects in the humanities. Some linguists, for example, are historians of languages; others work quite closely with philosophers. It also has links with the 'social' sciences, especially sociology and anthropology. Yet it has its 'science' side too, in the study especially of the sound of speech and how it is produced and perceived. Many have come to university with a vague idea of what it might mean to read, for example, Modern Languages, and have found in two or three years that this side of linguistics was what really fascinated them.

Boundaries between 'science' and the 'humanities' are in the end no more than a distraction. For what is the study of language but a 'science', practised once more by insiders, of something that lies at the heart of being 'human'?

Chapter 2
'*Homo loquens*'

From a linguist's viewpoint *Homo sapiens*, the 'rational' or 'knowing' species, is above all *Homo loquens*, the 'talking' species. No other aspect of behaviour is so strikingly peculiar to man (*Homo*).

Our nearest living relatives are two species of chimpanzee and the gorilla; then the other apes and, beyond them, other primates. These are animals whose behaviour can be watched and heard on TV, and is at times very noisy. Their calls, however, seem to form a limited repertoire. They also communicate in other ways, through facial expressions, hand movements, touch, and so on, and in that respect, at least, our species is still like them. Where we differ is precisely in the role of language. In Fig. 2 a female chimpanzee is seen quietly picking ticks or insects from another chimpanzee's hair: this is behaviour that primatologists call 'grooming', and who grooms who famously depends on social standing and the alliances or friendships that each animal forms with others. Now think, for comparison, of two women who are close friends. They might be cooking a meal together, and that itself is part of the continuing relationship between them. It is unlikely, however, that they will be silent. If they are married they may talk about their husbands or their children; they may plan a visit to the seaside, or discuss some intellectual topic that bears no direct relation to anything else they are doing. Where the micro-fabric of chimpanzee society is maintained by grooming, that of '*Homo loquens*' is maintained above all by speech.

What was the origin of this behaviour that is now so central to us? The genus *Homo* also includes earlier species now extinct: *H. habilis*, which is the first assigned to it, has been identified by fossils in eastern and southern Africa dating back 2.5 million years. Still earlier fossils belong to a line of 'hominids', or primates that are more 'man-like' than 'ape-like'. This form of vocal communication may not, therefore, have developed only in our own species, which emerged much later, or in its own immediate ancestors. Its development has nevertheless been very rapid. The hominid line was separated from that of the chimpanzees no earlier, on evidence that includes so-called 'molecular clocks', than 5 to 8 million years ago. That, as the processes of evolution go, is not a very long time. Yet we are talking about major differences between surviving

2. **Grooming in chimpanzees.**

species that must have originated in this period, and perhaps one even shorter. Were the changes that gave rise to language gradual or sudden? What advantages and costs might they have had? How much can we know, or guess, about what actually happened?

The structure of speech

Language is vocal. To be precise, it has evolved as primarily vocal, in an animal that cannot have been at crucial risk from predators through being heard while chattering. In the last 5,000 years it has also been written, and in societies like ours writing has a life of its own. Even today, however, in countries we call 'civilized' or 'developed', many people are effectively illiterate. No one would describe us as the 'writing' species, '*Homo scribens*', rather than the 'talking'.

We should be careful, therefore, not to think of speech as if it simply had the properties represented in our own or other writing systems. It is often, for a start, quite closely integrated with non-vocal behaviour. While talking, people smile or scowl; may beckon, or point at things they are referring to; may move their heads or do things with their hands in ways that are not random. Some gestures, like the one made innocently enough in Fig. 3, could be interpreted differently in different societies. Speech itself may be appropriately loud or quiet, rapid or deliberate, high-pitched or low-pitched. Imagine a mother calling by name her child, Peter, who is playing outside. He hears her, but perhaps pays not the least attention. She may then repeat his name, but in a more insistent tone of voice: possibly louder, with the vowels both longer and produced at a more level pitch, or with the overall pitch lower. The tone of voice is also central to a 'grooming'-like role, in maintaining family ties and friendship. Ordinary talk is often closely coordinated, in pitch and rhythm and loudness, among people who know each other well. A novel or a film script, for example, can at best hint at such features.

3. A hand gesture. The subject is simply beckoning impatiently: 'Come on! Hurry up!'. But would it always be interpreted in that way, in all parts of the world, in all contexts?

Nevertheless, the ones that speech and writing tend to have in common are the most significant.

The most obvious is that speech includes words. In more general or more neutral terms, its structure distinguishes repeated individual units with repeated individual meanings. The same unit *Peter*, for example, can be used to refer to the same individual in many different combinations, after *likes* in (in writing) *She likes Peter*, after *at* in *She looked at Peter*, before *likes* in *Peter likes her*, and so on.

Words, in turn, have their own structure. *Peter*, for example, can be analysed as spoken into a consonant [p] (*p*), followed by a vowel [iː] (*e*), followed by [t] (*t*), followed by [ə] (*er*): with stress added, [ˈpiːtə]. These smaller units will again form other combinations: [p] with, for example, a following [ɪ] in [pɪt] (*pit*); with a preceding [iː] in [hiːp] (*heap*); with a preceding [ɒ] and following [ə] in [ˈkɒpə] (*copper*). As such, however, these do not have individual meanings. Language therefore has two layers of structure. Units that have meanings form specific combinations on one level, and they in turn include specific combinations of still smaller units, which in themselves are without meaning.

No vocal structure like this seems to have evolved in chimpanzees or any other living primate. It is the key, moreover, to the remarkably efficient system of communication that our species now has.

We can see this best by trying to imagine simpler systems. The simplest of all would have neither 'words' nor units such as vowels and consonants. Imagining it does not perhaps require much effort: it would to that extent be like the repertoires of 'calls' distinguished in other primates. Like them, it would at best be seriously limited.

The calls could, individually, be complex. One individual might point, for instance, to another and produce a low-pitched growl whose pitch then rises. This might signal, say, that 'he' or 'she' is sick. To communicate that 'he' or 'she' is being naughty, one might produce instead a high-pitched giggle. To communicate that one is oneself sick, one might produce a series of barks followed by a sigh, and so on. Yet the differences would be between calls as wholes only. In the last example, the barks are not on their own a unit with a meaning 'I'. The sigh, in turn, does not have a meaning 'sick'; for 'he' or 'she' being sick there is no sigh.

Could such a system be successful? It is implicitly unlike primate calls in that, to distinguish signals like these, the repertoire would have to be much larger. How then could that be achieved? One way, in principle, would be to rely on ever finer differences: some growls, for instance, might be at a higher pitch or might be longer than others, some communications might have five barks and some six. The need, however, is not merely for distinctions, but for ones which will ensure that signals are not easily confused. The finer the differences, the greater the risk that they might be. One might, for example, mistake a low growl in a juvenile for a higher growl in adults, or miss one bark in a series. Another solution would be to make the utterances longer or more complex. But that too faces a limit, if the complexity is not to develop into something like that found in actual language. Think especially of warnings: what in other species are 'alarm calls'. They must be clear but, obviously, they should not be too long. It seems more efficient to have a single call that signals that some scary land animal is somewhere in the vicinity (which is the kind of thing that actual primate calls do seem to signal) than several calls that would distinguish, by the time one has got to the end of them, a lioness at running distance in grass on the left, or a pack of six hyenas straight ahead.

The obvious alternative (to us) is to distinguish separate 'words' for lionesses, grass, and so on. Let us therefore imagine another system which to that extent is similar to language; but the words do not in turn have smaller units such as vowels and consonants. A statement that Peter is sick might, for example, have two parts: low growl ('Peter') plus giggle ('sick'). To say that Mary is happy, one might produce a bark ('Mary') plus a whistle ('happy'). To say instead that Peter is not sick, one might add a rising growl at the beginning: rising growl + low growl + giggle. To say that Mary is not happy, one would add the same growl in the same place: rising growl + bark + whistle. Yet none of these growls or the like would have within it smaller distinct units, like the [p] or [iː] of *Peter*, forming new words in new combinations.

This is clearly, from our human viewpoint, an improvement. The problem, however, is that if the stock of words is too large, there is again a danger that they may be misheard. How many growls or barks or whistles would the system be able to distinguish before the signal that Peter was sick risked getting confused, when everyone was talking at once, with a signal that the baby was crying or his brother out hunting? Or before the words themselves got too long?

We do not need to answer these questions to appreciate why the system that has actually evolved is more efficient. A unit such as *sick* or *happy* is made up of smaller units which are individually combined in umpteen others, still short. The vowel and consonants of [sɪk] (*sick*) will make up, in a different order, [kɪs] (*kiss*): the square brackets again enclose transcriptions in the International Phonetic Alphabet. A shifting of the stress ([ˈ]) in [bɪˈləʊ] (*below*) will form [ˈbɪləʊ] (*billow*). They do not combine, however, in just any order: a word in English can begin with, for example, [sk] (*skin* or *skill*), but not [ks]. Even then the possible combinations are so many that not one need have a meaning: English has no word *zick*, for example, alongside *sick* and *zip*. It is also important that these smaller units have no meaning on their own. *Sick*, *zip*, and so on all have the same vowel, [ɪ] (*i*). But its role is simply to distinguish one word from another: *sick* from, for example, [sɒk] (*sock*), *kiss* from [kʌs] (*cuss*), or *billow* from [ˈbɛləʊ] (*bellow*). Nothing in the meanings of the words as wholes is correlated with it.

Redundancy

This last feature is important above all in ensuring that the structure of speech is sufficiently 'redundant'. A physical structure, like a bridge, is redundant in an engineer's sense if it is built with more components than the minimum needed for it to stay rigid. The advantage, of course, is that it will not fall down if one component cracks or is broken. Redundancy is likewise built into the hardware, for example, of computers: they will still work when, inevitably, there are failures in some circuits. The advantage of redundancy in language is that speech is rarely misheard, and the role of smaller units such as [s] and [ɪ] is crucial to it.

One fantasy that goes back for millennia is of a 'language' in which forms of words do systematically reflect their meanings. In English, for example, some words both begin with *gl* and refer to phenomena of light: *glow*, *gleam*, *glitter*, or *glare*. This is not carried through consistently, since many words without *gl*, such as *shine* and *dazzle*, also refer to phenomena of light, and many with *gl*, such as *glove* and *gloat*, do not. Let us try, however, to imagine a system in which similar forms and similar meanings do go regularly together.

The box overleaf shows just a fragment. A word begins with *n* if it is used of physical objects; one which is used of something abstract might begin instead with, say, *m*. The first vowel, *e*, appears in words for physical objects that are specifically of the vegetable kingdom, and a following *b* in those for ones that are edible. All the words, then, in our sample begin with *neb*. There are then distinctions between vegetables in the ordinary sense (*a*) and fruit (*e*), between bulbous vegetables (*p*) and green vegetables (*t*), between soft fruit (*s*) and fruit with stones (*f*). Only through the last vowel are specific kinds distinguished. This is not, in fact, pure fantasy but is inspired by part of an actual project devised by George Dalgarno in the 17th century. It is obvious, however, that it would be less efficient than the kind of system that has actually evolved. Think, for example, of a shopper trying to buy fruit and vegetables in a noisy market. One might ask for a kilo of nebapa (onions). But if a single vowel or consonant was misheard, one might easily get a kilo of garlic (nebape), or of sprouts (nebata) instead. Such mistakes are far less likely to happen in real language. Of the corresponding words in English, only *strawberry* and *raspberry* are partly similar, and only because both end in [bərɪ] or [brɪ]. The chances that *a kilo of onions* (['ʌnjənz]) might be confused with *a kilo of garlic* (['gaːlɪk]) are negligible.

Nor can words in real languages be used in any order; nor, within words, are the consonants and vowels combined in every possible way. That means still greater redundancy. Take, for example, the words *a bad meal*. In ordinary, rapid speech, the [d] of *bad* and [m]

21

Why are words not like this?

nebapa	'onion'	nebesa	'strawberry'
nebape	'garlic'	nebese	'raspberry'
nebapi	'leek'	nebesi	'grape'
nebata	'sprouts'	nebefa	'cherry'
nebate	'cabbage'	nebefe	'plum'
nebati	'spinach'	nebefi	'apricot'

of *meal* may overlap: look in a mirror, if you are doubtful about your own speech, to see when the lips close. Although [d] has been produced it could itself, in principle, be heard as [m], or as [t] or some other consonant; in the extreme case, not at all. What is said could not, however, be *a* [bam] *meal* since there is no word *bam*. It could not be *a* [ba] *meal* since not only is there no word [ba], but [a] cannot in any case end a word without a final consonant. It could not be, for example, *a* [bat] *meal* since, although there is a word *bat*, it does not make sense in this combination. Even if the [d] is totally obscured, what is said could only be *a* [bad] *meal*.

The redundancy of language is so great that writing systems often show just one part of its structure. A reader must be able to distinguish units like words, but one obvious method to represent them is as wholes. We use this method, for example, in arithmetic: 2 (read [tuː]) + (read [plʌs]) 3 (read [θriː]), and so on. It is also the basis of the system used for Chinese (see Fig. 4), though individual characters can be complex in a variety of ways. Other systems represent in principle the smaller units of which units like words are made up. Among them is, of course, the alphabet, and in modern practice words are then distinguished by the spaces between them. These spaces, though, are strictly more a help than a necessity. Fig. 5, for example, illustrates how Latin and Greek were

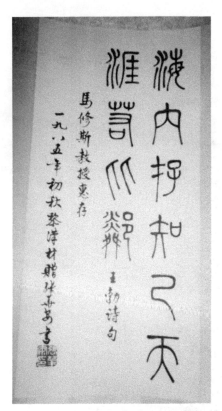

4. A Chinese scroll. The main text, in the form of calligraphy called 'seal script', is a couplet from a celebrated poem by Wang Po (7th century AD). The characters read in columns from top to bottom and from right to left, and each represents a unit of meaning which can be given its own gloss: first couplet *hai* 'seas' + *nei* 'within' ('in this world') *cun* 'preserve' ('live on') *zhi* 'know' + *ji* 'self' ('[people who] appreciate one'); second couplet *tian* 'sky' *yai* 'margins' ('the margins of the sky') *shi* 'is' *bi* 'group of five households' + *lin* 'neighbour' ('close neighbours'). The wording is allusive and laconic, in a literary style much valued in the society for which Wang Po was writing. The meaning is to be understood, however, as 'so long as' X (first couplet) 'then' Y (second couplet). In a free translation: 'Yet as long as true friends continue to exist, the ends of the earth are as close neighbours'. This fine example of two forms of calligraphy was presented to me, an ignorant westerner, by a visiting scholar.

5. A page from a Latin Bible. The sentence between punctuation marks in lines 10–13 of the first column reads: *ut omnis / qui credit in / ipso non pe/reat* 'that everyone who believes in him may not perish'. Note the line division in the middle of the last word (*pereat* 'may perish'). The manuscript was written in the 7th century AD, in letters of the type called 'uncials', and is in the Vatican Library.

written in manuscripts for centuries, exactly as if a modern publisher weretotrytosavepaperbyprintingbookslikethis. The structure of language is so redundant that we can still read it, and that is indeed how people who were trained to do it did read, slowly and, originally, aloud.

How might 'Homo loquens' have evolved?

Can we say anything with confidence about the origin of language? One current theory starts from the role of grooming (Fig. 2) in the social behaviour of related species. In many other primates social groups are quite small, and, so long as they do not get too large, this is an efficient means of forming and maintaining relationships. Human societies, in contrast, are not small, and the suggestion is that over time larger groups evolved in which relationships were maintained instead through complex forms of verbal behaviour. 'Language' was a more effective way of holding such societies together.

'Language', however, must be put in inverted commas. Complex forms of vocal behaviour are not necessarily language as we know it, and, if language-like forms of communication may have had that role in the beginning, what has since evolved has many others. There is no strict analogy between language, not now in inverted commas, and anything we observe in other primates. Nor are there evident homologies. Homologies exist where similar features have a common evolutionary origin: human arms, for instance, are homologous with the front legs of quadrupeds. There are also homologies in behaviour, in the calls of primates, among others, whose lines have been separate for longer than ours and the chimpanzees'. Analogies exist where features that may have a different evolutionary origin have similar functions: a bat's wing, for example, is analogous to that of a bird. Our basic problem is that, where language is concerned, there are no similarities of either kind that we can latch on to. It is therefore difficult to rule out any plausible theory. Some have even suggested, for example, that the

25

structure of language originally evolved in complex kinds of gestures, and that it was only later that a similar complexity developed in a spoken form.

A less speculative question is what kind of evolution we are primarily concerned with. In other species, there is little doubt that behaviour is in part genetically inherited. For some we know that it is also, in part, learned through experience: one kind of evidence for this can be seen when behaviour varies from one troop of monkeys, for example, to another. Beyond that, however, behaviour is explained by genetic evolution. Individuals behaving in certain ways have had greater reproductive success; their offspring have inherited their genes and behaved similarly, and so on.

In the case of language we are insiders, and are well aware of what can only be learned through experience. If I grew up speaking English, it is because my experience as a child was of people around me who themselves spoke English. If a baby of English-speaking parents was to be adopted and taken to France by a French-speaking couple, it would as readily, with the same genes, grow up speaking French and not English. One is not genetically 'programmed', as it were, to speak English, French, or any form of speech in any particular community. Our problem then is whether that is the whole story. Particular languages are a product of 'cultural' evolution, of cumulative interactions within human societies, independent of genes. To what extent, despite that, has the structure of speech in general evolved through genetic inheritance?

There are two independent ways to approach this question, neither at all easy. One way is to ask how language is now learned by children. Can we explain its development entirely by a process of learning through experience? In the view of Noam Chomsky, in particular, we cannot. The crucial period in which speech develops is quite short, and in normal children it develops uniformly, with few even relative failures. What develops is remarkably complex, especially in the patterns in which units like words are combined.

These vary greatly across languages, but certain kinds of pattern always seem to be excluded. The question then is whether that can be, in any strict sense, learned. The experience of language actually available to children is no more than what they hear, what is said to them, and how people react when they themselves speak. Although there is 'learning', this does not amount to systematic 'teaching'. Yet adults know not just how words can be combined, but also that specific kinds of combination are impossible. Is the input from experience a sufficient basis for this?

The answer, according to Chomsky and many linguists who have followed him, is no. There must, in addition, be a set of abstract principles of language which are strictly not learned but genetically inherited. The development of language in a child is thus to be explained by interaction of the input from experience with the structures these principles determine.

If Chomsky is right, the basic puzzle is the evolution of these structural principles, through genetic changes. 'Language-like' behaviour could still have evolved in earlier species: perhaps as early as *H. habilis*, whose fossils are associated with stone tools. Language as we know it must, however, have evolved in *H. sapiens* alone. In one seductive view, language first appeared in a particular population that palaeontologists classify as 'anatomically modern'. This population can be dated back some 100,000 years, and with it structurally modern language would have spread across the globe, as all other *Homo* species or subspecies lost out through their failure to compete successfully. The time-scale for its evolution is so short that, in one extreme view, we are forced to posit chance genetic changes.

The opposite way to approach our problem is to find out whether language could, in principle, have evolved through cultural processes. One method, therefore, is to run computer models of a population, in which individuals communicate with one another under constraints such as those implied in this chapter. There might be built-in pressure both to maximize the variety of messages that can be transmitted and to minimize their length, while again maximizing redundancy. As the population changes, it could also be constrained to maximize the ease with which a system can be mastered by new members. A computer simulation could then run for any number of generations, and the question would be how far language, or particular features of it, could evolve by gradual adjustments that would tend to optimize communication. One simulation, for example, argues that three-way distinctions among vowels, between an '[i]'-like sound, an '[u]'-like sound, and an '[a]'-like sound, could have emerged in that way.

Did language originate just once or more than once? That question too has often been asked, and the answer must be that, the more we posit rapid changes in genetic inheritance, the more it makes sense to assume a single origin. The more, however, we posit cultural evolution, the more talk of 'an' origin may mislead us. Our last near relative in Europe was the species (or subspecies) *H. neanderthalensis*, which became extinct a few tens of thousands of years ago. Neanderthals may well not have had a 'language', under a strict definition: it was argued in the 1970s that their anatomy did not, for a start, allow a range of vowels like ours to be distinguished. Under a wider definition, however, we can make a reasoned guess, from archaeological evidence of other kinds of behaviour, that they did. It is also possible that some general properties of language could have first emerged, through pressure to communicate effectively, in different human populations.

'The proper study of mankind', in the words of Alexander Pope, 'is man'. The line is sometimes torn from its context ('Essay on Man', II, 2); 'presume not', in contrast, 'God to scan'. For many linguists, their proper study is the structure of language as it now is, and it is presumptuous to suppose that we can understand how it evolved. But to think about the problem is at least a good way to appreciate what has made our species so remarkable.

Chapter 3
Language in time and space

The words people use are never fixed for all time. *Grotty*, for
example, was a new word when it was coined in Britain in the
1960s, and the usage of many speakers of English who were alive at
that time has changed to include it. *Gay* in the sense of 'homosexual'
seems to have had its origin in prison slang, and in 1950s Britain
could still be explained, in a passage cited in *The Oxford English
Dictionary*, as 'an American euphemism'. It has since become
familiar, however, even in the speech of many older people who,
when they were young, had known it mainly in such phrases as *gay
bachelor* or as Wordsworth used it ('A poet cannot but be gay') in his
poem about daffodils. *Wireless* or *wireless set* were normal terms in
Britain, for speakers young in the 1940s or 1950s, for what is now a
'radio'. The use of *wireless set*, especially, is now vanishingly rare,
even in the speech of people who once used it commonly.

This is not the only way in which speech changes. The accents heard
in old films, such as 'Brief Encounter', or in old recordings, such as
the announcement by Neville Chamberlain of the beginning of the
Second World War, would be quite unnatural in the speech of
anyone alive now. On a longer time scale, we can study written texts
reflecting speech in earlier periods. These show not just that every
language does change, but that changes are of many different kinds,
and that ways of speaking can, over time, change beyond
recognition.

Look, for example, at the first sentence in the box opposite. It is obviously in English: there is no need to translate it and, if the young woman who wrote it could be resurrected, her accent might not be so strange that we could make no sense of what she was saying. Nevertheless her language is not wholly ours. If she were alive now she would probably not say *diverse*; nor does *message* typically have the sense it had then, of a verbal communication sent through a messenger. Nor would *again* be used, as it is used here, to mean 'in return'. Her phrasing too would be a little different. *Had*, in particular, would now come after *never*: *I never had*, or, still better, *I have never had*. *Answer* now needs some word such as *an* before it: *have never had an answer*, or *have never had any answer*. Yet this is from a perfectly ordinary letter (of which we have many) of that period.

Now look at the second sentence. This again is 'English', in the sense that forms of English spoken now have developed gradually, over a thousand and more years of change, from this and other forms then current. Once we know this we can see, for instance, that *heofonum* must be an earlier form of *heaven* or *heavens*, and, knowing the now largely obsolete word *hallowed*, we may just about make that out in *ʒehalʒod*. But to read Old English one must learn it just as one might learn, for instance, to read German, and if the people who spoke it could be resurrected only a specialist who was very well prepared might have the faintest hope of understanding anything they said. Nor would Dorothy Plumpton have made much of it, although she lived far nearer to their time.

As language changes over time, so it varies from one human population to another. English is different from French or German, and still more from Japanese or Navajo. It can itself be spoken with a Scottish or Australian or other accent. Such facts are so obvious that it is tempting to take them for granted. Why is it, however, that while language (singular) is the same for every member of our species, languages (plural) are so very different? Why is it

Sentences in Middle and Old English

I have sent you diverse messages and writings, and I
had never answer again.

(Late Middle English, from a letter by Dorothy Plumpton to
her father, mid-15th century. The spelling has been
modernized. The term 'Middle English' is used of texts in
English roughly between 1100 and 1500.)

þu ure fæder þe eart on heofonum sy þin nama
ʒehalʒod.

(Old English, beginning of the Lord's Prayer, in a version
from around 1000. *Heofonum*, for example, would have
sounded roughly like, in phrasebook style, 'hair-von-oom':
in IPA ['heəvonum]. The first word (IPA [θuː]) is an earlier
form of *thou*: compare *du* in German. *Sy* ([syː]) is the
appropriate form of the verb 'to be' (lit. 'be thy name
hallowed'). The term 'Old English' is used of texts before
1100: thus, in particular, before the conquest of England by
French-speaking Normans in 1066.)

that two different speakers of a language such as English, who can
understand each other with no difficulty, may not speak exactly in
the same way?

The immediate answer is that variation is a product of change. The
English of St Boniface (or Winfrith), who converted much of
Germany to Christianity in the 8th century, would have been much
closer to the language of his converts than, more than a millennium
later, any form of Modern English is to any form of Modern
German. He was, in the general term that he himself used when he
was writing Latin, 'German'. Go back five centuries earlier, to a time
before the English tribes migrated into Britain from the Continent,
and the variation would have been more clearly among dialects of a

common language. Since then, however, the two populations have been largely separate. As their forms of speech changed, they changed independently. Therefore the languages in turn have separated.

Variation is not only geographical. If someone who speaks English also speaks German, their behaviour will be different in this way from that of someone who speaks only English. There will also be a variation in their behaviour, depending on which language they are speaking. If they first spoke English in their childhood and spoke German later, their behaviour changed as they did so. If eventually they speak German more than English, their behaviour again changes. These points are so obvious that they scarcely seem worth making. But speech also varies across dialects and accents, and there the case is much more interesting.

Variation in detail

We can understand this best through an example, which has as its centre what was in its day a pioneering study of the English spoken in New York in the 1960s, by William Labov.

The background to this illustration is the difference, within English, between accents with an 'r', and others without 'r', when not followed by a vowel. After *o*, for example, words like *sport* or *pour* have an *r* in the spelling, and this would once have represented [r], in an IPA transcription of speech, throughout the area in which English was spoken. It still represents an [r], whose quality varies audibly, in Scottish English or in what linguists describe as 'General American'; also for many speakers in, for example, the southwest of England. Thus, for the majority in North America, these words are phonetically [spɔːrt] and [pɔːr], and there is a difference between, for example, *pour* (with 'r') and *paw*, phonetically [pɔː] or [paː], (without 'r'). There is also a difference between the ends of words like *shiver* ([ˈʃɪvəʴ]), where the final vowel sounds 'r-like' or 'r-coloured', and *Shiva* ([ˈʃiːvə]).

There was a change, however, in the English of southern Britain which we know was well established by the later 18th century. In the form now normal, *sport* ([spɔːt]) rhymes with *ought* ([ɔːt]), and *pour* and *paw* are both [pɔː]. An 'r' in *pour* will show up when it is followed by a vowel, in *pouring* (['pɔːrɪŋ]) or, for example, *pour out* (['pɔːr'aʊt]). It can also appear, however, in a word like *pawing* or *drawing* (['drɔːrɪŋ]), even though in earlier periods, as reflected in the spelling, these words never had one. It is still more usual for a word like *Shiva* or *America* (['ʃiːvə], again, or [ə'mɛrɪkə]) to have a 'linking r', as it is called, when the next word begins with a vowel: [ə'mɛrɪkər'ɪz] (*America is*), rather than [ə'mɛrɪkə'ɪz]. When they do, they are again no different from such words as *shiver* and *butter*, which had 'r' historically: ['bʌtər'ɪz] (*butter is*). In this accent these too are without [r] when not followed by a vowel: ['ʃɪvə], ['bʌtə].

Map 1 gives a rough indication of the extent to which this partial loss of 'r' is found in local dialects. The change also spread to coastal cities in the east of North America, which had been colonized earlier, and was carried later into the forms of English that developed in Australia, New Zealand, and South Africa, from the 19th century onwards. It is clear that we could guess a great deal of its history, even if we now knew no more than how forms without 'r' are distributed.

A map, however, is at best a simplification. Map 1, to repeat, is of the distribution over local dialects. It therefore represents the speech, in any given area, least influenced by English as it is spoken anywhere outside that area. We should not read it, therefore, as suggesting that, at the time the survey was carried out, all people living outside the striped area pronounced an 'r' in such words, while everyone within it did not. That would have been nonsense then, as it is now. To talk of a single change is also a simplification. We could try to discover the routes by which this loss of 'r' spread from one group of people to another. Did individuals, however, who had regularly pronounced 'r' in the past suddenly, at some moment

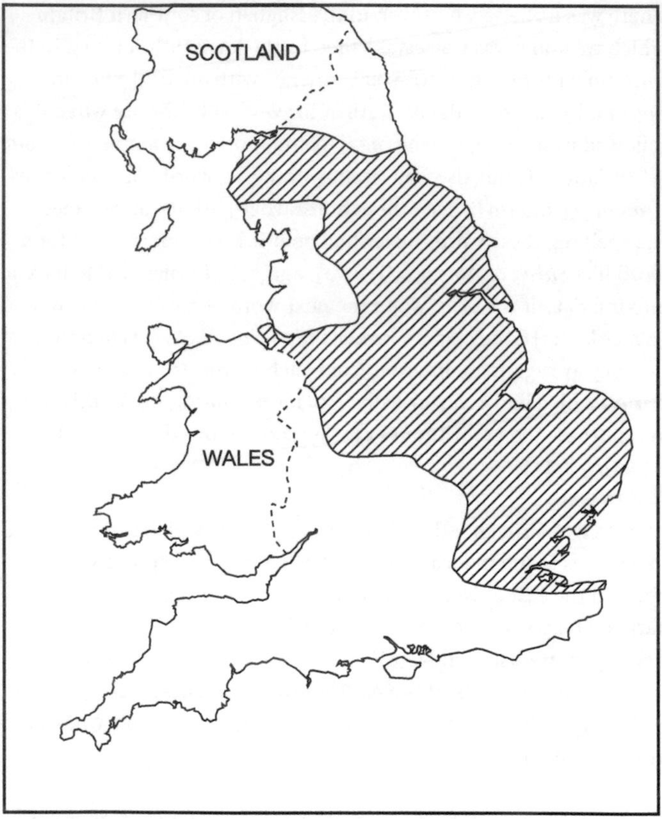

Map 1. English dialects without [r] at the end of a syllable. The striped area, without [r], is continuous. From a map by Jack Chambers and Peter Trudgill, based on the *Survey of English Dialects*, by Harold Orton and others.

in their lives, start to pronounce it no more? That is hardly plausible. But what might, in detail, have been true?

Labov's work in the 1960s came as an eye-opener. What it showed was not just that an individual's speech may vary. That might be expected from experience or common sense. The point was that it varied systematically, and not just when there was evidence that changes like this were in progress.

The English spoken in New York City had been studied by other linguists, and the history of 'r' in such words was in part known. Earlier in the 20th century it was not in general present. This was one area, therefore, where the pattern found in 'General American' had not held. By the 1950s it was clear, however, that things were not so simple. Many people native to the city did at times pronounce 'r' and at other times they did not. In that way there was variation, as again one might expect when speech is changing. The question, then, was whether it was random. If not, what exactly was happening?

In Labov's account, the frequency of 'r' was tied in with its social status. Its presence was, in his terms, a 'prestige' feature: the more one pronounced it, the less uneducated or of lower social status one would sound. He therefore expected it to be more frequent at a higher social level; also, for example, to be more common in careful speech, especially at that level, than in casual conversation. The change was what Labov called change 'from above'. It took place least or slowest at the lowest social levels, where people would be under minimal pressure (for the sake of their career, for instance) to produce prestige forms. At the highest level, people who were then old might once have pronounced 'r' rarely. They would now, however, be those under the most pressure to do so. Since the change was still quite recent, 'r' should also not just be more common at that social level, but most common of all in younger speakers.

Much of this was confirmed by the simplest of studies. Labov chose three New York department stores, one up-market, one down-market, and one in the middle. He simply visited each and asked the staff of all three, up and down the building, where he could find a department that he knew was on the fourth floor. Mostly, therefore, they would answer with the words *fourth floor*, both with potential 'r' or 'no r'. Each time he pretended not to have heard, and, by begging pardon, got them to repeat the direction more emphatically. Now he had anticipated that, the more up-market the store, the more salespeople would pronounce prestigious 'r's, especially in more careful or emphatic speech. Even, however, if we allow for possible subjective judgements, his hypothesis was strikingly confirmed. There was actually a difference, in the up-market store, between staff on the ground floor, which was more mid-market in appearance, and on the upper floors, with the snootiest staff and goods at the height of fashion. There were also, even in this study, differences between older staff and younger.

A later study involved a series of interviews, in part structured and in part artfully unstructured, of people living in the Lower East Side of the city. This largely confirmed what he had found. It was designed, however, to examine not just 'r', but five other points on which New York speech was known to vary. One, for example, concerned the initial consonants in words like *thing* or *then*. They were often realized as [t] and [d], as indeed by many people (whether or not they would admit it) elsewhere in the United States; alternatively, as [θ] and [ð] (= British English [θɪŋ], [ðɛn]); or, in between, in a way transcribed as [tθ] or [dð]. There was no evidence, in this instance, of a change in progress. Here too, however, there was variation both in and between the speech of individuals, which again reflected both their social status and the care with which they were speaking.

Studies of this kind have been repeated in other places, many, many times. Where there is variation among speakers, even without change, they suggest potential for change in the future. All it would take is for one variant to become more frequent; it might then, eventually, oust the others.

Where there is change, conversely, there will usually at least be detailed variation among speakers. It seems very likely, for example, that the frequency of *wireless* in the sense of 'radio' would at one time have been found to vary systematically with, among other things, the age of speakers. Four or more centuries ago, *not* could easily come after a verb: *It hurted not*, where one would now say *It did not hurt*. So could, among others, *never* (as in Dorothy Plumpton's *had never answer*); and, in a related pattern, Shakespeare could still write, for example, *What ring gave you, my lord?*, where the only normal form would now be *What ring did you give?* (*The Merchant of Venice*, V.1, 184). The changes seem to have come to a head in Shakespeare's lifetime, before and after 1600. Again, however, people did not just stop saying one thing and start saying only another. There is evidence in literature and documents of this period that usage varied strikingly, as common sense would lead us to expect, for more than half a century. Strictly speaking, it still varies. J. R. R. Tolkien, who was among other things a professor at Oxford expert in the earlier stages of the English language, could make effective use of sentences such as: *To that the Elves know not the answer* (*The Lord of the Rings*, V.9). This is certainly English – just no longer ordinary English.

Why does language change?

It is a fact, attested everywhere, that language changes. That is the reason why two languages which were once one, such as English or German, can in time become so different. It must also be the reason why there are 'languages' (plural) at all.

This last fact is, if we stop to think about it, quite remarkable. We are a single species and if any of us hears people talking in an unfamiliar language, it is clear at once that that is what is happening. Yet, without a language in common, people can communicate at best through gestures, smiles, and so on. This is an odd thing: that language (singular) has evolved as the main means by which human beings communicate, but because there is this multitude of languages (plural), each of us is actually able to communicate effectively with no more than a fraction of our species. How did that come about?

Let us assume, as many do, that language had a single origin. It evolved in one small species or subspecies, whose initial range lay, it is generally thought, in part of eastern Africa. In time, however, the population expanded, across Africa and into Europe and Asia; from Asia to Australia and into North America; from North America to South America; finally from Asia once more into the Pacific. Map 2 represents one educated guess at roughly how and when this may have happened, based on at least some indirect evidence. Whatever the details, however, it is obvious that as the range expanded different groups of human beings would remain in contact only with the others in their immediate area. Let us then assume that, in the original population, language had within it features that could change. That means, in effect, that it was not determined genetically in all respects. As people separated, how they spoke would start to vary independently; as they separated further, it would change yet more; therefore, in populations that no longer had the slightest direct contact, language could take ever more divergent forms.

Hence the Babel that the ancient Hebrew scriptures explained by divine interference. Within limits that might be genetically determined, language (singular) diversified by gradual changes, over a few tens of thousands of years, into the precursors of the languages (plural) which, after further movements of people to and fro, we can observe now. We have to assume that from the very beginning it had the seeds of variability within it. Why, however, did change have to follow?

One answer is put into the mouth of Adam in Dante's *Divine Comedy*. The words translated in the box are those of a poet of the early 14th century, but can easily be updated. Language itself is 'natural' in that it is an inherited characteristic of our species. Particular forms of language are, in contrast, aspects of the culture of specific human societies. But such societies never stand still. We make continual changes in the precise cut of our clothes, in the

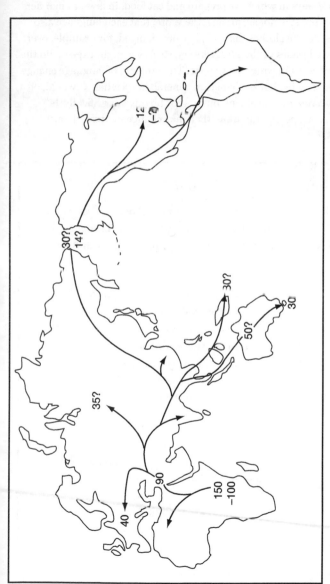

Map 2. How the range of *Homo sapiens* may have expanded. The dates (in thousands of years before the present) are tentative and depend in part on the assumption that 'land bridges' had to be available at times when sea levels were lower.

precise ways in which we prepare and eat food, in laws, in manners, and so on. It is not surprising, therefore, that each language also varies. As the clothes that people wore changed, for example, over the ten decades of the 20th century, so, as we might expect, did the precise ways in which they spoke. The problem of language change would thus be that of change, in general, in societies. It would, of course, remain a problem, but not for linguists specifically. Is change in speech at bottom, then, like change in dress or eating habits?

How Adam explained it

The Bible says that the earliest human language was created in the Garden of Eden. But it had already disappeared, as Adam explains, before the building of the Tower of Babel:

> For never yet did product of man's reason
>   Remain unchanged, because of mortal taste
>   Which changes ever, following the season.
> Simply that man should speak is nature's deed;
>   But how you speak, that nature leaves to you
>   As best may suit with your immediate need.

Even the name of God himself changed:

> Ere I descended to the world of woe,
>   J was the earthly name of that supreme
>   Good whence the joy comes that enfolds me so;
> El was his next name and that well befits,
>   For mortal custom is as leaf on branch
>   Which falls and then another follows it
>
> (Dante, *Paradiso*, XXVI, 127–138,
> translated by T. W. Ramsey)

The idea is certainly tempting. Fig. 6 is a portrait of the most distinguished British linguist of the late 19th century. Note, among other things, the way his necktie has been knotted loosely; also his shirt collar, which is starched very stiff and would have been attached with studs in front and at the back. Fig. 7, in contrast, is a portrait of a distinguished British linguist of a later generation. This is still not how a man of his age and in his position would dress now, but it is much more like it. Both Sweet and Jones were linguists with a marvellous ear for English as they heard it spoken, and we know that, over their joint lifetimes, that too was to change. The vowels of *poor* and *moor*, for instance, were once separate from those of *pour* and *more*. They were instead, as dictionaries still transcribe them, [pʊə] and [mʊə]. These vowels are still distinct, of course, in many other forms of English. But in southern Britain they now tend to be the same: *poor* and *pour* are both [pɔː]; *moor* and *more* are both [mɔː]. The change has naturally been gradual, and over many years the speech of many individuals will have varied. So, in any period, would their collars and ties

Our interest, however, is not simply in describing individual changes, but in explaining why they take specific forms in specific circumstances. As most linguists see it, they are never isolated. We are dealing not just with a single vowel or single word; not even, for example, with a single pattern of word order. Every change, in principle, has repercussions elsewhere in the language, connecting it to others that are also in progress, or may follow later. For many linguists, these connections reflect fundamental laws to which a language – any language – must be subject. If the appeal to laws is valid, then linguistic history is exciting history indeed.

Even if it is not, one thing well worth remembering is that mastery of speech develops early in our childhood. The speech of adults does, of course, change: when, for example, they start using a new word or they move to a new place and their accent adapts to their surroundings. Nevertheless the structure of their language is in large part fixed before their teens. At the age of two, children are

6. Henry Sweet (1845–1912). A great phonetician and scholar of the English language. His 'Anglo-Saxon Reader' has been repeatedly re-edited for the use of students.

7. Daniel Jones (1881–1967). The grand old man of phonetics in the United Kingdom, responsible more than any other for the principles that underlie the International Phonetic Alphabet.

typically beginning to put words together; a few years later they are already speaking with the right forms, in the right order, recognizably in a language they will speak from then on.

Hence, for many linguists, change in language is essentially from one generation to the next. Children of any generation master forms of English, for example, from the speech they hear around them in the communities in which they are brought up. That basically determines how they speak it for their lifetime. A language changes, in one common analysis, when the children of a later generation, as they in turn hear speech in the community around them, master it in what is partly a new form. Our basic problem is to understand how that can happen.

There is no consensus on these issues. But it does seem that the way a language changes is not quite so simple or uncontroversial as a change in fashion in such things as collars and ties.

Chapter 4
Language families

I once read a book by someone who thought it a great mystery that, at one point in their history, the people of Italy stopped speaking Latin, a language they had been happy with for centuries, and started speaking Italian instead. Why should they have done such a thing, and how did they manage it?

We can see now that there was no mystery. Speech is forever changing and, as Old English has developed by gradual changes into modern English, so the language that is now Italian, which has been written for most of the last 1,000 years, evolved, again by gradual variations from one generation to the next, out of the one spoken, some 2,000–2,500 years ago, as Latin. There was no striking switch, no single point at which one could say: here the earlier way of speaking ended, here a new way began.

But, as Latin changed, it also split up. It was originally the language of a small state, centred on Rome. But the Roman ruling class was good at and addicted to war, and by around 2,000 years ago had established a great empire, whose western provinces included not just Italy, but all of what is now France, Spain, and Portugal. Throughout this area, Latin increasingly replaced the existing languages. Within 500 years it was doubtless varying already from one region to another, much as Spanish, for example, varies across South and Central America. By then, however, the western empire was politically in ruins. It was therefore natural that, as contacts between people became rarer, the Latin spoken in different regions tended to change independently. Fast forward 500 more years, and a language that had once been unified had fragmented into a myriad of local varieties, which at any distance were clearly different. One variety, in origin specific to the Tuscan region of north central Italy, was to become Italian. Another, in a region centred on Paris, later developed into modern French; another, from Castile in northern Spain, into Spanish; and so on.

Images can always mislead, but in cases like this, as in the development of species in biology, it is natural to think in terms of ancestors and families. Latin, in this image, is the 'ancestor' of a family of languages 'descended' from it. These descendants include French, Spanish, and Italian; also, among national languages, Portuguese and Rumanian. In zoology, the cat family includes lions, leopards, domestic cats, and so on. In linguistics, these languages are the leading members of the 'Romance' family.

In zoology, the cat family is then grouped with others in still wider classifications, as a family of placental mammals, of mammals generally, of vertebrates, and so on. Ask any specialist in linguistics, and you will be similarly told not just that the Romance languages descend from Latin, but that they and it once had an ancestor historically still more remote, in common with a host of others. Romance is no more than one branch in a family tree of 'Indo-European' languages (Fig. 8) whose twigs, as it were, extend across much of Eurasia. Now we cannot say exactly how a single ancestor came to have descendants in such widely separated places. No single theory is accepted by all prehistorians. We do know, however, that there are other families, elsewhere in the world, whose members are distributed very widely. As linguists we are also certain that, for all the Indo-European languages, a single ancestor must once have existed.

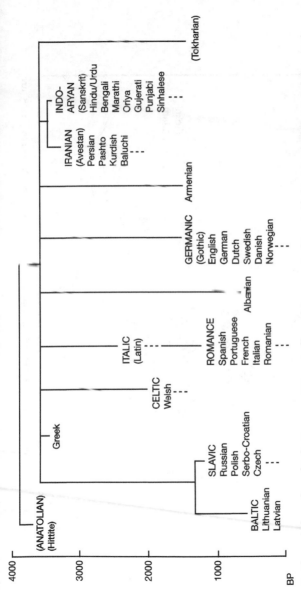

8. The main branches of Indo-European. Names of branches as opposed to specific languages are in capitals; names in brackets are of languages and branches either dead or whose descendants are now named differently. Indo-Aryan and Iranian together form a larger branch called 'Indo-Iranian', a larger 'Balto-Slavic' branch is still disputed, as too is the precise relation of Anatolian to all the others. The scale on the left indicates approximately when each branch is first attested by substantial material.

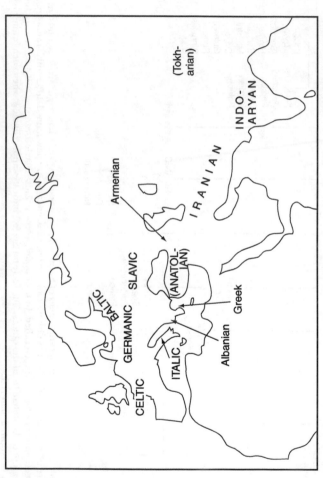

Map 3. The historical distribution of Indo-European. The locations of dead branches (Fig. 8) are again in brackets.

How, though, can we be certain? I will give dates 'BP' (for 'before the present'), and, on this scale, the earliest evidence we have of any branch of Indo-European is from around 3,500 BP, for Greek, written in the script called 'Linear B', and a little earlier for Hittite, which was the language of an ancient empire with its capital in what is now north central Turkey. The first evidence for Latin is between 2,000 and 2,500 BP; for Sanskrit, which is an ancient language of northern India, we have oral poetry whose origins are earlier than 3,000 BP. Nowhere, however, do we have the slightest direct evidence of a common ancestor. Writing itself was not invented, for any language, until a little over 5,000 BP, and the earliest evidence is of Sumerian, in what is now the south of Iraq, which is not of this family. Even the earliest of these languages, moreover, were less like each other than, for example, Spanish and Italian are today. Why are we so confident that they were prehistorically related?

What is our evidence?

The answer lies in the 'comparative' method. This involves a step-by-step comparison of different languages, in which we look for detailed correspondences that cannot reasonably be explained unless a common ancestor existed. The great problem is: what sorts of detail are convincing?

We can perhaps get some feel for the argument if we concentrate on just two phrases, in the box overleaf, in just two Indo-European languages. The one in Greek appears in Homer's *Iliad*, a narrative poem whose origin is before 3,000 BP, in a passage where the hero, Achilles, is faced with a hard choice. If he fights in battle he will gain 'imperishable fame', but at the cost of his life. If he does not fight he will return home safely, but his 'noble fame' will be lost. (He is the hero and, naturally, he fights.) The one in Sanskrit appears in a collection of religious poems called the Rigveda, whose origins are also from before 3,000 BP. The same translation fits both, and in the view of many scholars the whole phrase was inherited not just

49

> ## Corresponding phrases in two Indo-European languages
>
> | *Ancient Greek*: | kléos | ápʰtʰiton |
> |---|---|---|
> | *Sanskrit*: | ʃrávah | ákʂitam |
>
> | fame-NOM/ACC.SG | NEG-perishable-NEUT.NOM/ACC.SG |
> |---|---|
>
> 'imperishable fame'
>
> Both phrases are transcribed with symbols from the International Phonetic Alphabet. A raised 'h' distinguishes 'aspirated' consonants ('pʰ', 'tʰ', 'kʰ') from 'unaspirated' (p, t, k); the *ʂ* in *ákʂitam* is pronounced like 's', but with the tip of the tongue bent back towards the roof of the mouth. The acute accent marks a point at which the pitch of voice is higher. The glosses (third line) are explained in the text.

from a common ancestral language, but from what was once a common poetic tradition. There are only two words; but it is fascinating to discover just how many correspondences they illustrate.

Let us start with their grammar. Both languages distinguished what grammars call 'genders', by which words like those for 'fame' are classed (as in, for example, German) into 'masculines', 'feminines', or 'neuters'. Both *kléos* (Greek) and *ʃrávah* (Sanskrit) were neuter. Greek and Sanskrit also had distinctions (as in German or Russian) between what grammars call 'case'. In Greek, for example, if one said that a man did something, the word for 'man' would take the

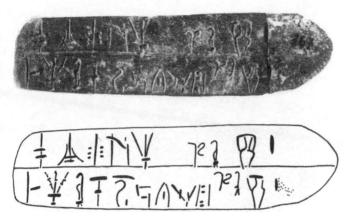

9. The earliest evidence for Indo-European (1): A tablet in 'Linear B'.
The text dedicates (first line) 'To all the gods one jar of honey'; (second
line) 'To the mistress of the labyrinth one jar of honey'. It is one of many
tablets excavated at the ancient site of Knossos in Crete, known in
Greek myth for the labyrinth, or maze, inhabited by the Minotaur. The
'code' of Linear B was famously cracked by Michael Ventris in the
1950s, applying techniques of decipherment learned in the Second
World War. The spelling basically is syllable by syllable: thus *pa-wi*
(first two characters in the first line) 'to all'; *me-ri* (immediately before
a picture, in both lines, of a two-handled storage jar) 'honey'. Syllabic
writing is a type distinct from both an alphabet, in which consonants
and vowels are represented separately, and a script directly
representing units with meanings, as in Chinese. It is at present used for
Japanese especially, in the scripts called 'katakana' and 'hiragana'.

form *ánthro:pos*, with a final -*s* distinguishing it as in the
'nominative' case (NOM), and as 'singular' (SG), referring to one man
only. If one said that someone else did something to a man the word
would take instead the form *ánthro:pon*, with a final -*n*
distinguishing an 'accusative' singular (ACC.SG).

Now look at the words for 'imperishable'. These too had to be
neuter, in 'agreement', as grammars put it, with the words for
'fame'. This is the 'NEUT' in their gloss, which again fits either
language equally. They also had to be in the same case. Here,
though, there is another parallel. The word for 'man' in Greek was

§43

10. The earliest evidence for Indo-European (2): A cuneiform text in Hittite. 'Cuneiform' means 'wedge-shaped' and refers to a form of writing widespread in the ancient Near East, made by pressing a point sideways into clay. It was adapted to Hittite from Akkadian, which was the language of Assyria and Babylon. The tablet of which this is a part sets out the laws of the Hittites, detailing appropriate penalties for very specific offences. Paragraph 43 (marked) reads: 'If a man usually makes his ox cross the river and another person pushes him away and takes the tail of the ox and crosses the river, and the river carries away the owner of the ox, then they take that person.' The tablet dates from the century before 3,500 BP, making this one of the earliest texts in any Indo-European language.

masculine, and distinguished, as we have seen, a final 'NOM.SG' -*s* from an 'ACC.SG' -*n*. But in neuters 'NOM' and 'ACC' were never distinguished: hence the 'NOM/ACC', in the words for both 'fame' and 'imperishable', in the glosses. That held for Sanskrit too; and moreover, in either language, many neuter 'NOM/ACC' singulars had an ending identical to that of the 'ACC' form found in many masculines. Thus, in the phrase in Greek, the word for 'imperishable' also ends in -*n*: *ápʰtʰito-**n***, like *ántʰro:po-**n***. Similarly for a final -*m* in Sanskrit: *ákṣita-**m***, like, for example, *su:nú-**m*** 'son-ACC.SG'.

52

These similarities are suggestive, at least. We then find more cases, however, where an -*n* and -*m* again match. A form like Greek *kunô:n* 'of dogs' was in a 'genitive' (or 'of') case, with a genitive plural ending -*o:n*. The corresponding word in Sanskrit was *śúna:m*, also a genitive plural with the meaning 'of dogs'. This has the ending -*a:m*. Only the specific vowels and consonants are different: Greek -*n*, Sanskrit -*m*; Greek -*o:n*, with a long *o* (IPA ':'), Sanskrit -*a:m*, with a long *a*.

Another still more obvious correspondence is at the beginning of the two words for 'imperishable'. Both have a negative meaning: literally 'non-perishable'. This is the 'NEG' of the gloss, and in both words, and in others like them in both languages, we find an initial *a*-. Now it is also easy to find points where Greek and Sanskrit appear not to correspond. Even there, however, what is normal in one language may still find a parallel in a form that is unusual in the other. Greek had a normal ending -*o:*, for instance, in forms such as *ékʰ-o:* 'I have' or *leíp-o:* 'I am leaving'; comparable forms in Sanskrit had a different ending -*mi*. But -*mi* is also found as an exception in Greek, in a small set of forms like *eimí* 'I am': compare Sanskrit *ásmi*.

Why should there be such correspondences? These languages were spoken thousands of miles apart, in societies historically separate. We can therefore imagine the excitement when the evidence from Sanskrit first became known in the West. Just as French and Spanish, for example, had a common ancestor in Latin, so the astonishing thought arose that languages like Greek and Sanskrit also had one, spoken by some population deep in prehistory.

If this is right, the -*mi*, for instance, which we find in a few forms in Greek must be a survivor of the same ancestral ending as the -*mi* in Sanskrit, where it either remained or became normal. How certain is it, though, that we are right? Could correspondences like these be due instead to pure chance? Or is some other scenario possible?

The last question is not rhetorical. We know, in particular, that when the speakers of two languages are in prolonged and frequent contact, both their grammar and the words they use tend to change in ways that make them similar. Is it possible, then, that Greek and Sanskrit had no common ancestor; but, at some stage in their separate prehistories, they were spoken by two neighbouring populations? Could that scenario explain why forms like these, even ones irregular in at least one language, should correspond so widely?

Reconstruction

To rule it out, we must develop an account so detailed, comprehensive, and consistent that no other can be reasonably accepted. We therefore need to look quite carefully at the logic of what we are proposing.

What we are claiming, for example, is that -*n* in Greek (in words such as *ápʰtʰito-n*) and -*m* in Sanskrit (in words such as *ákṣita-m*) both have the same source. This was perhaps itself *n*-like, or *m*-like, or perhaps not quite like either. That then is a specific hypothesis, and it concerns the 'reconstruction', as an entity that hypothetically existed in prehistory, not just of a phonetic unit, but also of a grammatical ending, in forms that hypothetically underlie 'ACC' and neuter 'NOM/ACC' singulars. If the preceding vowels are also relevant, they too must have a specific prehistoric origin: *ápʰtʰiton*, *ákṣitam*. So, for example, if the words as wholes are also relevant, must the consonants that follow the initial *a*-: *ápʰtʰiton*, *ákṣitam*.

It will be obvious that, in this logic, 'correspondences' need not be between forms that are similar. The words for 'imperishable' happen to be alike in some ways: the same number and structure of syllables, accents (high pitch) in the same positions, and some vowels and consonants, like the *i*'s and *t*'s in the words for 'imperishable', phonetically at least close. For the 'fame' words there is evidence, within Greek and Sanskrit, that they were once in part closer: *kléwos, fráwas.* In principle, however, similarities in individual forms are neither necessary nor sufficient. As languages change, vowels and consonants, syllables and accents change with them. The forms we reconstruct might therefore undergo quite striking alterations; but the forms that they gave rise to could still be explained, as our hypotheses develop, as successfully as any others.

Let us look, then, at the vowels in the words for 'fame'. Where the Greek form had an *e* (*kléos*), the one in Sanskrit had an *a* (*frávah*). So, however, did heaps of other forms that seem potentially related. Compare, for example, the words for '(he, she, it) is': Greek *estí*, Sanskrit *ásti.* Where the Greek form has an *o* (*kléos*), the one in Sanskrit has another *a* (*frávah*) 'fame'). So too the words for 'imperishable' (*áphthiton, ákṣitam*), and again many others. A Greek word like *éloipon* 'I was leaving' had an ending -*on*: *élcip-on*; an ending with a similar role in Sanskrit was, as we are beginning to expect, -*am.* In this light, we can now propose a hypothesis still more specific. In the common ancestor, the vowels in such forms were distinct: one probably *e*-like and the other probably *o*-like. In Greek they stayed separate, but in the prehistory of Sanskrit they both became *a*.

Of the consonants in both words, the *t*'s in *áphthiton* and *ákṣitam* 'imperishable' were, of course, phonetically similar. What matters, however, is again not that, but that this correspondence too is general. Compare once more, for just one instance, Greek *estí* '(he, she, it) is' and Sanskrit *ásti.* The *k* in the Greek word for 'fame' (*kléos*) is, in contrast, not remarkably like the *f* in Sanskrit (*frávah*). The same consonants correspond again, however, in the words for 'dog': compare once more Greek *kunô:n* 'of dogs', Sanskrit *fúna:m.* Another instance, famous in the history of Indo-European studies, is in the words for 'hundred': Greek *hekatón*, Sanskrit *fatám.* If the changes implied seem at all unlikely, then note, for example, that the word for 'to sing' in Italian also begins with a consonant that is phonetically a [k] (*cantare*), which corresponds to [ʃ] in French: *chanter*. We can also, to resume, find other instances where Sanskrit has an *r*, as in *śrávaḥ*, but Greek (and the languages of other branches) have *l*. Hypothetically, the consonant at this point was originally *l*-like.

In the end there will, of course, be loose ends. Alongside the words for '(im)perish(able)', we can find a handful of others in which *kṣ* in Sanskrit corresponds to *pʰtʰ* or something like or partly like it in Greek. Yet exactly how these fit in is not clear. Why too, for instance, did the Greek word for 'hundred' have a *he-* at the beginning (*hekatón*)? The issue, however, is not whether the theory we are proposing explains everything. Common sense suggests that we will never be able to do that. It is whether, for what our hypotheses do cover, any other form of explanation, which does not posit a common ancestor, is even remotely plausible.

How far can we go?

Findings like this are of great interest to prehistorians in general. We are not sure how the Indo-European family came to be so widespread. As linguists we believe, however, that there was a common ancestor, and the problem then is to find relevant evidence from archaeology. An archaeologist, however, is often able to link prehistoric cultures by much simpler correspondences: by similar pots or swords, say, found in graves. It is therefore natural to wonder whether linguists need to plunge into such detail. Should we not be able to find similarities so striking that, in any reasonable judgement, it is clear at once that languages must have a common origin?

On the contrary, we must get the message that this is a field of serious (and in itself quite fascinating) research, where the slotting in of detail after detail is essential. Even similarities that stare us in the face might be misleading, if they do not have their place in an extended network of hypotheses.

Take, for example, the word in Latin for 'to have': *habeo* 'I have', as it is entered in dictionaries. The *hab-* is similar to English [hav] (*have*), or the identically written *hab-* of German *haben*, also 'to have'. At first sight, this is just the kind of correspondence that should be significant. The similarities, in both form and meaning, are so close that it seems they must go back to the same source.

In fact, we are quite sure they do not. All three languages are Indo-European, English and German from the 'Germanic' branch (Fig. 8). It has been known, however, for the best part of 200 years, that there are widespread differences in consonants when Germanic is compared with Latin or with other branches. Where the Germanic languages have *h*, Latin has instead *c* (phonetically [k]). Compare (with other changes) German *hundert* 'hundred', Latin *centum*; German *Hund* 'dog', Latin *canis*; German *Hals* 'neck', Latin *collum*; German *Hure* 'whore', Latin *carus* 'dear' in the sense of 'loved'. These correspondences are part of a much wider picture, in which the *b*'s of *habeo* and *haben* prove equally misleading. The form in Latin which we actually believe to have the same source as the *hab-* in German had both different consonants and a different meaning: *cap-* (*capio* as entered in dictionaries) 'to take hold of'. So too the forms in German or in English that share their origin with *hab-* in Latin: German *geb-en* 'to give', English *give*. The 'sameness' that so hits us at first sight of these words is in reality an accident of prehistoric changes in both sounds and meanings.

Such examples serve as a grim warning never to rely on isolated or sporadic correspondences. They also warn us, indirectly, that the further back we try to reach into prehistory, the less hope we have of demonstrating anything.

The reason, once more, is that languages change. Their grammatical structure changes: neither English nor, for example, Italian still have elements related to the genitive plural ending, or the neuter 'NOM/ACC' endings, of Sanskrit or Greek. Their vocabulary also changes: old words are progressively replaced by new ones; old meanings shift or disappear. There will therefore come a point at which a family relation cannot be recovered. We may feel in our bones that it is there. Form *a* in one language may well look like form *b* in another, and form *c* in that look like form *d* in a third. But there is no longer the evidence that justifies a detailed and connected reconstruction, and, without that, we just do not know. For any similarity or set of similarities, we have always to discount alternative explanations: that they are accidental, that they reflect a prehistoric contact among people whose languages were not immediately related, or a combination of these.

Where confidence shades into speculation is a matter of judgement, and specialists in some conjectural families take a rosier view than others. We must nevertheless hold fast to the logic of our argument. Linguists have no equivalent of a zoologist's fossils, stretching back beyond the earliest records of writing. An archaeologist's pots and swords are also genuine records of their period, at worst broken or reduced to rust. Our evidence, however, is entirely of the forms that have developed after languages have split up, often transformed by their history.

It is remarkable, therefore, how much linguists have been able to reconstruct. For a final illustration, let us go back to the changes that affected consonants in Germanic. One upshot, as we have seen, is a correspondence between German *h* and Latin *c*. Another can be illustrated, to take one example, with the words in Sanskrit and Germanic meaning 'brother'. 'Gothic' (for linguists) is the earliest known Germanic language, in an early translation of part of the Christian Bible. Compare then Sanskrit *bráːtar-* 'brother' (this is again transliterated with the symbols of the IPA) with Gothic *broθar*. But Indo-Europeanists were soon faced with a problem. Take, for comparison, the form in Sanskrit meaning 'father'. It too had a *t* as its middle consonant: *pitár-*. In Germanic, however, the words for 'brother' and 'father' developed different consonants: *broθar*, with a *θ*, but *fadar*, with one usually transliterated *d*. The two consonants are still different, after yet more changes, in modern German: *Bruder, Vater.* What can have lain behind this?

The answer was discovered in the 1870s, by a Danish scholar called Karl Verner. He told people that it occurred to him one afternoon when he was unwell and trying to get some sleep, with a comparative grammar of Indo-European to assist him. Suddenly the Sanskrit forms for 'father' and 'brother', which were printed in bold type, leaped out at him. The first, he noticed, had an accent on the second syllable: *pitár-*. The other had it on the first: in the transcription I have given, *þrá:tar-*. Could that have something to do with it? When he checked the evidence thoroughly he found that this had to be the explanation. No Germanic language has a direct trace of what would once have been the Indo-European accent. We deduce it from, in particular, Sanskrit and Greek. The hypothesis nevertheless was that, in the prehistory of Germanic, it must still at one time have been there. It then meshed with the consonant changes, and only later was it lost. The editor of the journal in which Verner published his paper wrote to him that he had brought light into places where everyone before had walked in darkness. This may seem over the top; but, if there had been any doubt about the reality of the relations among Indo-European languages, the reconstruction of a change so evidently prehistoric would have dispelled it.

Chapter 5
In praise of diversity

In 1492 Christopher Columbus first set foot in the West Indies.
Thus began a series of events that brought disaster to the peoples of
the New World, and to most of the languages spoken by them.

Others soon followed. In 1500 Brazil was claimed for the crown
of Portugal, and a Portuguese governor-general was appointed
31 years later. In 1519 Hernando Cortes began the Spanish
occupation of Central America, and in 1533 Francisco Pizarro
overthrew the Inca Empire in the Andes. In 1607 the first successful
English colony was established in North America, under the
leadership of John Smith, in Jamestown, Virginia; in 1608 the
French colony in Québec was founded by Samuel de Champlain.
Nearly two centuries later, in 1788, the British started their takeover
of Australia. There too, as in North America, the overwhelming
majority of people now speak English. Elsewhere in America, more
than a hundred million now speak Spanish or Portuguese.

Across most of the Old World, languages of other families, or other
branches of Indo-European, are still dominant. Over a hundred
million speak Arabic, or Hindi and Urdu, or Bengali, or the
standard (Mandarin) form of Chinese, or Japanese. Many other
languages, such as Tamil or Vietnamese or Javanese, are native to
tens of millions. A linguistic survey of the world can be divided, if
we are realistic, into two parts. One covers the continents of the Old

World with their adjacent islands, where the distribution of languages and families is still largely as it was 500 years ago. Even in sub-Saharan Africa, where English and French are widely known and many languages are disappearing, most people do speak one or more of them. The other includes three continents in which the indigenous languages have been swamped by ones originally from western Europe. A few that remain are locally important: Guaraní, for instance, is an official language of Paraguay, alongside Spanish, and, with Quechua, which was the language of the Incas, still has speakers in the low millions. Many other indigenous languages survive, more than most people who are not professional linguists realize. Many of these, however, are likely to disappear before long, as new generations fail to learn them.

For linguists, all languages are precious. The ones most readers will know are a biased sample, historically either European or from other regions of the Old World. The more biased it is, the more one is tempted to assume that every language, wherever it is spoken, must have structures similar to theirs.

At one level, languages are indeed alike. Our species first spread to Australia, for example, up to 50,000 BP; to North and South America from perhaps as early as 30,000 BP. These populations were then separated from those left behind, and their languages evolved independently for tens of thousands of years, until Europeans invaded. There is no difference, however, between any of them and any language of the Old World that we could not in principle explain by changes of the kind all forms of speech are liable to undergo, extended over greatly longer periods. And any other group of people could, in principle, speak any of them. In language too, *Homo sapiens* has remained one species.

At another level, many languages have evolved in ways that seem to Western eyes surprisingly exotic. This judgement is, of course, entirely relative. If human history had been different, linguists speaking American languages like Navajo or Tzeltal might instead

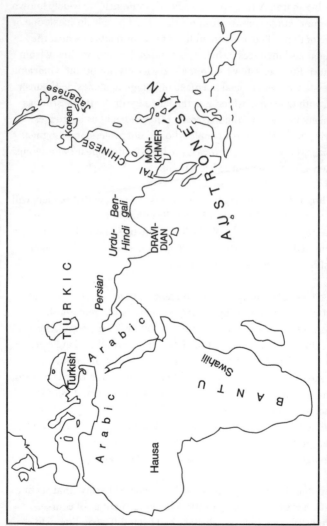

Map 4. Some major languages and families in Asia. The languages in italics are Indo-European. The extension of Austronesian especially is wider.

The main families of the Old World

Eurasia in particular is an area across which people have traded and migrated, and formed shifting empires, throughout history. The INDO-EUROPEAN family is one of three with members in both continents (see Map 3 in the last chapter). The others are a smaller group classed as URALIC, which includes Hungarian and Finnish; also TURKIC, which includes a range of languages related to Turkish, in what was once the south of the Soviet Union. The main language of North Africa and the Near East is now Arabic, whose expansion accompanied that of Islam. This belongs to the SEMITIC family, which can be linked to others, including the language of ancient Egypt, in the northern half of Africa.

On the mainland of east Asia CHINESE includes Mandarin, Cantonese, and others, and is classed as a family with others to the west, which include Tibetan and Burmese. Note that neither Korean nor Japanese is part of that or any other known group. DRAVIDIAN in South India is a smaller independent family, whose largest member is Tamil. MON-KHMER is also an independent family, which includes Cambodian (Khmer) and Vietnamese, as is TAI, which includes Thai. The large AUSTRONESIAN family is centred in the islands off Southeast Asia, where it includes Tagalog and the other languages of the Philippines, Malay, Javanese, and most others in Indonesia. It also expanded eastwards across most of the Pacific; and westward to Madagascar. Elsewhere in Asia smaller familes are established, for example in the Caucasus.

In the southern half of Africa the largest clearly established family is BANTU, roughly from the Equator southwards. Swahili, in East Africa, is its largest member and is still spreading.

be fascinated by the exotic character of strange tongues such as English, still spoken by a few old people in a remote part of Britain. Any feature, in any language, is potentially 'exotic' in comparison with those of other languages that do not have it.

What do languages distinguish?

One feature of English, for example, is a grammatical distinction between 'singular' and 'plural'. Words like *boy* (singular) or *woman* (singular) are in a form used in referring to a single individual: one boy, or one woman, only. Forms like *boys* (plural) or *women* (plural) are used instead in reference to two or more individuals. A similar distinction, between 'one' and 'more than one', is familiar in other European languages: Spanish *la mujer* 'the woman', but *las mujeres* 'the women'; French *la femme* (phonetically [la fam]), but *les femmes* ([le fam]); and so on.

But this is not the only distinction of which the human mind is capable. Why should singular as opposed to plural be so central to the grammar of such 'unexotic' languages, while other contrasts are not?

Take the sentence *I have picked some flowers*. Anyone who says this will be understood, since *flowers* is plural, to have picked two flowers at least. They could also, however, have been flowers of at least two different kinds: some gladioli plus some dahlias, these plus some lilies, and so on. Alternatively they might all be of the same kind: all gladioli, or all lilies. This difference too is clear and objective. Yet in English, in whichever case, an expression such as *some flowers* would be equally appropriate. Why should speakers of this language, and of others like it, be obliged to distinguish 'one' from 'more than one', but not also, or perhaps instead, 'one sort' from 'more than one sort'?

The question may at first seem perverse. Surely 'one' and 'more than one' are more important. Why, though, this 'surely'? Are they more obvious, or more vital to the needs of clear communication? Or is it simply that we happen, ourselves, to speak a language in which they have to be distinguished?

There are certainly languages in which a similar distinction need not be made. In Chinese, for example, speakers can quite normally use the same form to refer indifferently to more than one or one only. We can in turn find other languages, including many buried under English in the United States and Canada, with a grammatical element that linguists call 'distributive'. This distinguishes a set whose members are in some way differentiated: so, for example, forms that might be glossed as 'flower-DIST' could be used of flowers that, as well as being two or more, are not all of the same sort. If they were all gladioli or all lilies, the form would instead have no 'DIST'. 'Fish-DIST' ('fish of various species') could in turn contrast with 'fish' without 'DIST', meaning 'one or more fish of the same species'. Note the 'one or more'. For things to be of different sorts there must be at least two of them. A set whose membership is homogeneous may, however, have one member only. Distinctions between 'one' and 'more than one' are subsidiary and, again, may not be explicit.

Another perfectly objective difference is between things that can be seen and things that are invisible. The flowers, for example, might be in full view when the speaker refers to them; or they might be somewhere else or hidden. In either case, in English, one could say *some flowers*. However, in the Wakashan languages, a family whose remaining speakers live along the coast of British Columbia, this difference is subject to a grammatical distinction. In English, forms like *this flower* (singular) and *these flowers* (plural) can be distinguished, when appropriate, from *that flower* and *those flowers*. In Wakashan languages, contrasts like these are more complex and obligatory. One form that roughly corresponds to *this* means, more exactly, 'with or close to or connected with I who am speaking'; plus, if nothing is added to it, 'that can be seen'. Another means 'with, etc. you to whom I am speaking'; plus again, if nothing is added to it, 'that can be seen'. These forms are then distinguished from others, with an added element, used in reference to things that cannot be seen. Similarly for forms that broadly correspond to English *that*: 'the one(s) over there that we can see', as distinguished from, again with the 'invisible' element, 'the one(s) over there that we cannot see'. Note again 'one(s)'. Visibility is central; so too the connection or lack of it with an 'I' or 'you'. Distinctions between 'one' and 'more than one' need not be drawn.

These examples were first cited nearly a hundred years ago, by the American anthropologist Franz Boas. It is easy to add others, often from languages of which the world in general knows and cares little. It is therefore tempting, once more, to dismiss their features as 'exotic' or marginal. Again, however, they are not objectively 'less important'.

Look, for example, at Fig. 11. It shows a young woman wearing a sling, in the way she might do if she had broken her arm. In English, then, one might unthinkingly report this with some sentence such as *She has broken her right arm*. Is it certain, however, that she has done so? Suppose you have seen her in reality. Under examination, you might admit that, actually, she was simply wearing a sling. The rest is an assumption based on what you have seen, and could have been mistaken.

Here too we are dealing with distinctions that many major languages do not make. In English one is forced, for example, to distinguish an event entirely in the past from one that bears a relation to the time of speaking: *She had* ('have-PAST') *broken her right arm* as opposed to *She has*. One is not forced to distinguish further between forms we might gloss, in addition, 'have-PAST.KNOWN', or 'have-PAST.ASSUMED'. On other occasions forms like *has* are used in repeating things that one has heard from someone else. Again, however, there are no forms that distinguish 'have-KNOWN' from, alternatively, 'have-REPORTED'. Even when they

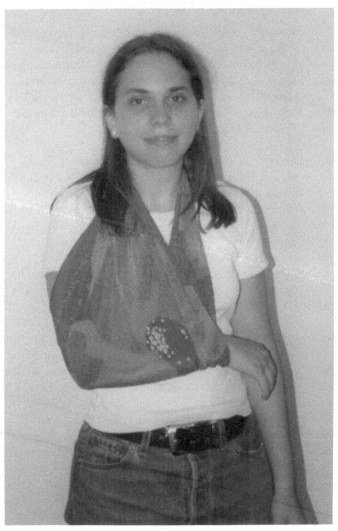

11. A young woman wearing a sling. Has she or has she not broken her arm?

are reporting no more than a rumour, people can still use the same expression *She has broken her right arm.*

There are other languages, however, in which glosses like these are not out of place. Assertions rely on different kinds of evidence; therefore it is only honest and natural, as their speakers might quite reasonably argue, that one should be forced to use forms with an 'evidential' meaning, that distinguish among them. How slack they might think languages like English are, whose grammar does not make distinctions of this sort!

Tuyuca, for example, spoken on the boundary between Colombia and Brazil, distinguishes as many as five 'evidentials' (see box). The distinctions are obligatory: speakers cannot make an assertion without clarifying whether it refers to something they have seen, or to something they have heard about, and so on. If they have seen it, they should use a form for evidential number (1), glossed 'VISUAL'. If they have merely heard about it, they should use instead a 'SECONDHAND' form, number (4). A speaker may, of course, lie; but there is no generalized equivalent of *She has broken her right arm*, with no evidential.

Let us now compare these with some other possibilities. In English, for example, statements like *I have a headache*, which are made by speakers who are talking about themselves, have a structure similar to that of statements about others: *She has a headache* or *They have their hats on.* The sentences are different, naturally; but *I have* differs no more from *She has* or *They have* than either of these differs from the other. Now, in Tuyuca, either of the last two statements could again report things that a speaker has been told. The evidential form would then be 'SECONDHAND', again number (4). A statement equivalent to *They have their hats on* might, again, refer to something that the speaker can directly see. In that case the evidential would again be number (1), 'VISUAL'. A speaker cannot, however, see their own or anyone else's headache. If it is their own they feel it, and the evidential in Tuyuca would be number (2) in

Some examples of evidentials in Tuyuca

There are five evidentials, identified as (1) 'VISUAL', (2) 'NON-VISUAL', (3) 'APPARENT', (4) 'SECONDHAND', and (5) 'ASSUMED'. They are distinguished by endings in conjunction with both 'past' and 'present' and a partial indication of 'I', 'you', and so on. Thus, in the first example, the ending -wɨ can be glossed, more precisely, by both 'VISUAL' and 'PAST', and is used in referring to, among others, the 'I' who is speaking.

(1) atí-wɨ   wáa-wi
    VISUAL   VISUAL
    'I came'   'He went'

Note: One can see oneself as well as someone else.

(2) mũtúru bisí-tɨ   tisá-ga
            NONVISUAL   NONVISUAL
    'The motor roared'   'I like it'

Note: A nonvisual form is also used of something that would have been visible, had there not, for example, been a wall in the way.

(3) bóahõã-yu
        APPARENT
    '(Apparently) I threw it away'
    (said of something found to be missing)

Note: 'Apparent' evidentials are rare in reference to the present, and logically excluded in statements with present reference to the speaker. One has direct knowledge, visual or nonvisual, of what one is oneself now doing or feeling.

(4) pũũyukí mãnĩ-yíro

    SECONDHAND

'There weren't any hammocks'

(said after hearing that a shop was out of them)

Note: A 'secondhand' form is used in stories and legends as well as in reporting what the speaker has heard recently.

(5) diágo tii-kú

    ASSUMED

'You are sick'

(judgement based on the way someone was groaning)

Note: An 'assumed' form will also be used in stating what can be known, for example, from the state of the world in general or from normal patterns of behaviour.

(From an account by Janet Barnes in the 1980s. A tilde (˜) is the IPA sign for a 'nasalized' vowel: compare, for example, French *on* ([ɔ̃]); [ɨ] is a vowel between [i] and [u].)

the box, 'NONVISUAL'. Someone else's headache cannot be experienced either visually or nonvisually. Nevertheless one might infer it from their appearance or the way they were behaving. The appropriate evidential might accordingly be number (5), 'ASSUMED'.

Such distinctions between evidentials are among the features linguists expect to find in the various languages of a large area of South America. English is among the many languages throughout the world that, from a Tuyuca viewpoint, 'lack' evidentials. That is hardly because they are not needed for precise communication.

It is simply that the histories of these languages happen to have been quite different.

Speaking and thinking

When different languages draw different distinctions, do their speakers still perceive the world around them in the same way? Or do people speaking different kinds of language think of it differently?

At one point, for example, I referred to 'sets' that might have just one member: just one flower, or just one fish. That is not, however, what *set* means in ordinary English. It is one of many words linked regularly to plurals: *a set of chairs, a group of several women, a bunch of these flowers*, and so on. But such words do not go with singulars: *a set of a chair, a group of one woman, a bunch of this flower*. Here, as elsewhere, the distinction between singular and plural is obligatory. There is no expression like (as it were) *a set of chair*, where *chair* would equally refer to one chair or to many. In speaking English, one is forced to talk about the world in terms of, on the one hand, single individuals and, on the other, sets consisting of at least two individuals.

To demonstrate that sets can have one member, it is therefore easier to switch to mathematical notation. Thus, if we take a set $\{a,b,c\}$, with members a, b, and c, and subtract from it a set $\{b,c\}$, with members b and c, the result must be also a set, $\{a\}$, which has the single member a. For beginners, however, this can still be something of a revelation. Might it be, then, that when someone has been brought up speaking English, they are predisposed to think in terms of categories, like 'one' as distinct from 'at least two', that it imposes?

If so, other kinds of language, that make other distinctions, might be seen as predisposing speakers to think differently. We must be careful, however, not to infer ways of thinking or perceiving from the evidence of languages alone.

71

In English, for instance, a sentence like *The colours are nice* has a structure similar to that of *The curtains are red*. *Colours* and *curtains* are words of one kind: each a plural with a corresponding singular (*colour, curtain*), both related similarly to other words before and after. *Nice* and *red* are both words of another kind: neither of them either singular or plural, both with forms that grammars call 'comparative' and 'superlative' (*nicer, nicest; redder, reddest*), each related similarly to *are* and, through it, to the other words. The grammar of English is, in this respect, like that of other major European languages. Words that are grammatically of the same kind are not, however, necessarily alike in meaning. *Red* identifies a physical property of material objects, like, for example, those that would be referred to by *the curtains*. *Nice*, instead, expresses a subjective judgement. *The colours*, too, would refer to physical properties of objects, not to objects themselves. It is not surprising, therefore, that in other languages the grammar may be different. Words with meanings such as 'nice' and 'red' may not have forms that are distinguished similarly, or relate to other words in the same way. *The colours are nice* might have to be translated by a sentence that, if glossed in English, would be more like 'It is nice in colours', or 'It colours nicely'.

Is someone brought up speaking English predisposed, then, to conceive of colours as like objects, or to think of 'niceness' as like 'redness'? Or is that merely how they have been predisposed to use words? The problem is one for philosophers and psychologists, not linguists alone. As linguists, however, we can point to cases where the evidence is more suggestive, at least.

One of the most interesting has to do with relative positions in space. One way, in principle, to represent them is by geographical coordinates: thus, in English, *Beijing is **north** of Shanghai*, or *Chicago is **west** of New York*. Another way is to refer to an intrinsic relation: thus, in English, an expression such as *inside* in *The pen is **inside** the box*, or *between* in *Mary is **between** Bill and Andrew*. A third way, which is very common in a language such as English, is to refer to a relation as seen from a specific viewpoint. Look, for example, at Fig. 12. From the viewpoint of the camera, one of two adjacent objects intervenes between it and the other: thus (as a speaker of English would represent it) *The glass is **in front of** the vase*, or *The vase is **behind** the glass*. To someone looking from a viewpoint opposite the camera, the relations of 'in front' and 'behind' would then be reversed. They would therefore be represented instead by sentences such as *The vase is **in front of** the glass*, or *The glass is **behind** the vase*. *To the left of* is a similar expression, whose opposite is *to the right of*. Thus the glass is to the left of the vase if they are viewed from a position to the right of the picture; from a viewpoint to the left, that too is reversed.

12. **Two objects on a table. What are their relative positions?**

Expressions like these are so normal in English that one is not generally aware of absolute coordinates. The photograph in Fig. 12 was taken, as it happens, with the camera due south: the vase was therefore to the north. If you had been there you might, conceivably, have known this; you might also, for example, have been able to say, if asked, that the vase was slightly nearer to the city centre. Neither, however, has any bearing on the way in which the relation between it and the glass would be represented. The only relevant coordinate is the subjective angle from which it is viewed.

Tzeltal, for comparison, is a language of the state of Chiapas in the extreme southeast of Mexico, for which I rely on accounts by Stephen Levinson. It too has many forms, like English *inside* or *between*, by which speakers can refer to an intrinsic relation. Tzeltal does not, however, have expressions such as *left* or *right*, *in front* or *behind*, which would refer to a subjective coordinate. What matters instead is an absolute coordinate of just the kind that, in the case of what is shown in Fig. 12, a speaker of English would ignore.

Levinson discusses, in particular, a dialect spoken in an area that drops steeply from a range of mountains, roughly to the south, with a valley to the north. Suppose, then, that a speaker sees one object standing to the south of another. They do not have to be within this territory; they might be on a plain, for example, well outside it. The objects, however, are related on an axis parallel to the way it slopes; therefore, from whatever angle the speaker views them, one will be referred to, in the most convenient gloss, as in a position 'uphill'. The other, to the north, will be 'downhill', and other objects, neither 'uphill' nor 'downhill', would, in relation to the same coordinate, be 'across'. For people to speak about the world in that way, they must constantly be aware of how they are oriented. Levinson reports, for example, that speakers of Tzeltal have been led into an unfamiliar concrete cell, with no windows, and could still point accurately in the direction of places where they had been, up to 100 miles away. The way they talk about positions in space obliges them to be dead-reckoners, in a way that speakers of a language such as English, who talk differently, need not be.

This is perhaps as much as linguists, wearing that professional hat alone, can contribute to this argument. But what we do know, certainly, is how wonderfully varied languages can be, in the categories they make explicit, in the kinds of words distinguished, in how their speakers talk in general about their world. That, just in itself, is a great eye-opener and mind-liberator.

Chapter 6
What is a language?

Earlier chapters have touched on the diversity of languages, on change in a specific language, on a language splitting up to form a family of languages. What though, exactly, is a language?

We are insiders and, for many purposes, we have a right to take this term for granted. We all know that English, for example, is one language and French or Arabic are others. Let us reflect, however, on these statements. We say that Chaucer's *Canterbury Tales* were written in English; the Koran in Arabic; the *Song of Roland*, from around the end of the 11th century, in French. Yet a speaker of modern French, for instance, would not understand the poet of the *Chanson de Roland* if they met in the street. We know that English is not spoken in the same way in, say, Glasgow and Jamaica; that the Arabic of Morocco or Algeria is different from that of Egypt or Iraq; that a film in French made in Canada may need subtitles in France. What then are these 'languages' that vary so much?

Obviously, they are abstractions. No single form of speech or writing is called, for example, 'English'. Instead there are many 'Englishes': that of Chaucer's England, or of Shakespeare's; that of Jamaica, or of the West Indies generally; that of South Africa, Australia, and so on. What then, in reality, is English itself?

Language and dialect

The quotation below registers the basic truth that no two people speak, in every detail, in exactly the same way. The context is the splitting of a language into dialects, that might, over centuries, develop into new languages. Italian and French, among others, have developed out of dialects of Latin. So too have many forms of speech that linguists still call 'dialects'. Are these truly different?

> We must in reality distinguish as many languages as there are individuals.
>
> (Hermann Paul, 1880)

Linguists are often asked, for instance, just how many languages there are. The answers they give tend to centre on around 5,000 to 6,000: in the thousands, certainly, but fewer than 10,000. Any estimate, however, is best taken with a pinch of salt. For what count as separate 'languages' for specialists in one part of the world are often much more like each other than the 'dialects' of a single language as described in others.

An Italian linguist, Giulio Lepschy, tells a story that bears on this problem. One day in Venice, which is his home city, he was sheltering from a downpour next to two girls who were speaking in a way he simply could not make out. It was not, he felt sure, any of the languages of the Romance, Germanic, or Slavic families he was familiar with; it did not even seem to be Indo-European. He therefore decided to ask them and, since he was in Italy, asked in Italian. They were rather surprised, but answered at once, in Italian, that they were speaking the 'dialect' of Roseto degli Abruzzi, half-way down the Adriatic coast of Italy, which was where they came from. Now this form of speech is one of many throughout Italy whose origins, like that of French or Spanish, or Italian itself, are in what were, over a thousand years ago, varieties of Latin. For specialists in Romance linguistics, it remains a 'dialect'. Nevertheless he, as an Italian from Venice, had not understood one word of it.

Why should it not be counted as a separate language? The short answer is that that is not how people in Italy describe it. The reasons, however, lie deep in their cultural history, especially in the status of Italian as a written language. 'Nothing is a language', as the scholar Pietro Bembo defined it in the 16th century, 'that does not have a literature'. But that criterion makes sense only in societies with a long tradition of literacy. If 'literature' means literature in writing, no 'languages' at all would have existed, in large areas of the world, until at best recently.

Boundaries between states can also influence the way these terms are used, as can broader ties of nationhood or ethnicity. Max Weinreich's brilliant epigram (below) was originally in Yiddish, a language (?) or a dialect (?) once spoken widely among Jews in Eastern Europe, though never that of a political unit. For many linguists, however, the essential test is how far people using different forms of speech can understand one another. This is a matter of degree, and depends in part on how far they adapt their speech, perhaps subconsciously, to make understanding easier. Nevertheless, by that criterion, the girls from Roseto degli Abruzzi were bilingual. They were speaking one language among themselves, and Lepschy spoke to them in another. Naturally they answered in that.

> A language is a dialect with an army and a navy.
>
> (Max Weinreich, 1945)

Whatever our criteria, 'dialects' too are obviously abstractions. Are we talking of a form of speech specific to Roseto degli Abruzzi, or of how large a territory that includes it? Remember that a form like 'New York English', as identified by William Labov, had striking variation within it. Our basic problem therefore concerns any form of speech in general, dialects included.

Languages as systems

It would be wise, in this light, not to get hung up on what we call things. Both 'dialect' and 'language' are terms applied to ways of speaking we perceive as different. There are many others: 'patois', for example, is a French term for a local form of speech distinguished within broader dialects; a 'creole', as linguists define it, is a form historically derived from an earlier 'pidgin'. Some 'languages', like Latin as it is still taught in Europe, are primarily not forms of speech, but written. Others, like the gestures used by signers, are not forms of speech at all. But, in any of these cases, what exactly are we studying, and what status has it?

One answer is that we are studying a system. This may not at first seem such a striking insight: any 'way' of doing something such as speaking might be said to be a 'system' governing how one does it. The idea, however, is that a linguistic system is determinate: we can say in principle exactly what it is and what lies outside it. Within it units form a self-contained set of relations: each linked, directly or indirectly, to each of the others. The formula below, which was originally in French, sums up this insight perfectly.

> A language forms a system . . . in which everything holds together.
>
> (Antoine Meillet, 1906)

The relations that form systems are in part of contrast. In English, for example, 'singular' contrasts with 'plural'. In Tuyuca, each of the five evidentials (see the box in the last chapter) contrasts with each of the others. If a word is in, for instance, an 'ASSUMED' form, that excludes the possibility that it has the meaning of a 'VISUAL' form, or of a 'NONVISUAL' form, or of an 'APPARENT' form, or of a 'SECONDHAND' form. The possibilities are just these, no indeterminacies blur them, and if there were four evidentials, say, instead of five, the network of relations would be different. In investigating any language one thing linguists look for at once are the sets of contrasts, like these, to be found within it.

Where forms contrast, however, we can also abstract rules. *Boys*, to begin with a simple illustration, is one of many English plurals ending in *-s*: phonetically, that is, [z]. It is therefore formed on what grammarians call a 'regular' pattern. 'Regular' has in origin the meaning 'by rule' (Latin *regula*), and in teaching foreign languages it often helps to make such rules explicit. Start from the singular, as the rule might say in this case: *boy*, for example, or *girl*. Then, if it is for written English, add *-s* to the end: *boy + s*, *girl + s*, and so on for all other words of this kind unless their plurals have to be learned individually. There is evidence, moreover, that a rule like this is not just the invention of linguists and language teachers. *Mouse*, for example, has the irregular plural *mice*: 'irregular' means 'not by rule'. To be precise, *mouse* has *mice* as its plural in its basic sense of 'rodent of the family Muridae'. In the sense, however, of 'device for moving a cursor' it quite normally has a plural *mouses*, as a further general rule ((2) in the box) predicts. Some experiments in the 1950s made use of a nonsense word *wug*, referring to a drawing of a bird-like creature. How, for example, would young children form a plural from it? Answer, as we would expect for words of this form, *wugs* ([wʌgz]).

Rules are also part, then, of the systems linguists describe. There are rules, however, not just for grammatical endings, like [z]. Many are instead for ways in which words are combined and ordered. Take the sentence *A young woman will be coming*. In place of *a young woman*, one would not say, for example, *young a woman*; nor, except allowably in old-fashioned verse, *a woman young*. Nor would one say *be coming will*, or *be will coming*; *Will be coming a young woman*, or *A young will be coming woman*. To explain why is to posit rules that people seem to follow when they are saying what they do say.

To suggest that rules are 'followed' is perhaps to risk a slight misunderstanding. People 'follow', for example, an explicit recipe or route map. They might thus explain, if asked, that when they add an egg, or turn left at a crossroads, they are following an instruction

How to form a plural in English

The most general rule, for English as it is written, is to add -s:
singular *boy*, plural *boys*. In this example, *s* represents [z]
([bɔɪz]); similarly in [klɔːz] (*claws*), in [rʌgz] (*rugs*), in
['wɛpənz] (*weapons*), and in many others. The rule for these,
then, is:

(1) Add [z] to the singular.

In writing, however, the ending can also be -es: singular *box*,
plural *boxes*. This represents [ɪz], which is found, more
generally, when singulars end in one of a specific set of
consonants. These include the [s] in *box* ([bɒks]) and the [z]
in, for example, *rose* ([rəʊz], plural ['rəʊzɪz]); also [ʃ] as in
bush ([bʊʃ], plural ['bʊʃɪz]), [tʃ], as in *church* ([tʃəːtʃ], plural
['tʃəːtʃɪz]); and [dʒ], as in *fridge* ([frɪdʒ], plural ['frɪdʒɪz]).
Such consonants are called 'sibilant', and we therefore add a
subrule:

(2) Insert [ɪ] between [z] and a preceding sibilant.

Finally, -s also represents [s]: thus [kats] (*cats*), [dɛsks]
(*desks*), or [klɪfs] (*cliffs*). In all these, the preceding consonant ([t], [k], or [f]) is of a class called 'voiceless'. We
therefore add a further subrule:

(3) Change [z] to [s] when a preceding consonant is voiceless.

(3) then applies in any case not covered independently by (2).

(These rules also cover a few plurals that are only partly
regular: for example, plural [liːvz], with regular [z] but [v]
(*leaves*), only partly matching [f] in [liːf] (*leaf*).)

given. Speaking, clearly, is not governed literally in that way. Suppose one asks: *Can Mary help?* If pressed to say why, one would not explain that, in a question, words like *can* must come first; or that one would break a rule by putting *Mary* after *help*. One simply takes for granted that a sentence like this will take that form.

Nevertheless each of the rules implied expresses a true 'regularity'. The way the first two words are ordered contrasts with the way they are arranged in *Mary can help*, which is typically a statement. A question *Will Bill help?* is different in the same way from *Bill will help*; *Could you come?* from *You could come*; *Was she here?* from *She was here*; and so on for as many pairs of sentences as we can think of. We can thus abstract a rule for questions and for statements generally, from an effectively endless set of similar contrasts. The other rule would exclude, for example, *Can help Mary?* There is no contrast here: the rearrangement simply makes no obvious sense. Neither, however, would *Will help Bill?*, or *Could come you?*, or *Was here she?*, or *Must put it on the table Peter?*, and so on, for all other combinations of this kind. The rule or rules abstracted apply, 'regularly' again, to all of them.

What speakers take for granted linguists therefore try to make explicit. Recall especially the redundant structure so essential to the efficiency of speech. To ensure this many combinations of its elements must be, literally, ruled out. That is, their exclusion must be regular. What they are will vary from one language to another, and the rules involved are real and central to each.

So what status have they?

Many linguists see this as the centre of their subject. Linguistics in the past half-century has been dominated by discussion of the kinds of unit languages distinguish, of the forms of rule they include, of how rules mesh with one another, of how the system as a whole is organized into subsystems. This forms the core component of most courses in linguistics, and the core too, sometimes the whole substance, of most current textbooks.

The way textbooks are organized reflects in part reality; also, in part, convention and ease of exposition. Let us reserve this, therefore, for the section at the end of this book which will suggest further reading. The problem that concerns us in this chapter is again the nature of such systems, or of 'languages', in general.

One view is that, in describing 'a language', we are describing structures present in speech, in what people say and could say. 'What people say' or 'could say' is already an abstraction. The language could be seen, however, as a set of ideal sentences, extrapolated from those heard from, or acceptable to, speakers. Noam Chomsky's definition in the 1950s is a classic formulation, and in practice this view is still fruitful.

> I will consider a *language* to be a set (finite or infinite) of sentences, each finite in length and constructed out of a finite set of elements . . .
>
> The fundamental aim in the linguistic analysis of a language L is to separate the *grammatical* sequences which are the sentences of L from the ungrammatical sequences which are not sentences of L and to study the structure of the grammatical sequences. The grammar of L will thus be a device that generates all of the grammatical sequences of L and none of the ungrammatical ones.

(Noam Chomsky, 1957)

Another view, however, sees the 'language' as the system itself. Take, as a starting point, two people who are judged to have a language in common. Since they share it, one of them might ask the other, say, to pass some object; the other hands it over, and in doing so, may speak and will be understood in turn. Exactly what they say will be

13. Ferdinand de Saussure (1857–1913).

Ferdinand de Saussure

Saussure (Fig. 13) is famous for a *Course in General Linguistics* (1916) that he never actually wrote. He had lectured on the subject three times between 1906 and 1911, but the book was composed by others after his death, largely from notes taken by his students.

It makes a strict distinction between individual acts of speech (French 'parole') and the language ('langue') shared by the members of a society. The language itself is a system with objective reality in this society. A second basic distinction is between a language as it exists in a given period, and its history from one period to another. Linguistics then has two main branches: one 'synchronic' ('simultaneous in time'), the other 'diachronic' ('through time'). A famous analogy compares the history of a language with the progress of a game of chess. To study it synchronically is to describe the pieces on the board at any moment between moves. To study it diachronically is to say how they have reached these positions.

Such ideas have dominated most work in linguistics from the 1920s until now. In more dated terms, Saussure spoke of a language as a system of, in French, 'signes'. In each 'linguistic sign', a 'signifier' (French 'signifiant') is coupled with something 'signified' ('signifié'). *Girl*, for instance, can be represented by the coupling of a mental impression of its sound ('[gəːl]') and a 'concept' ('girl'). Signs are established solely by distinctions between them and other signs within a system.

The term 'structural linguist', in use from the 1930s, refers especially to linguists who explicitly followed Saussure.

appropriate to what they are doing, to the object in question, to the way they are related socially, as close friends or possibly as people who have just met, and to many other factors independent of the language itself. Yet if they did not share the same words and the same rules by which words are ordered and contrasted, they would not be able to communicate in that way. The 'language' is this abstract system that, sufficiently at least to understand each other, they both have.

'Have', though, in what sense? One classic account is that of Ferdinand de Saussure (see box), in which the system common to such people exists in a whole community. This view comes nearest to the way a language such as 'English', or the dialect of Roseto degli Abruzzi, may appear to us before we start to worry about what it is. The answer, however, that most linguists might now claim to work with rests on subsequent accounts by Chomsky (see box in the next chapter). To speak a language is in brief to 'know' it, and the 'knowledge' of at least one will develop in each person in their childhood, in the mind of each child individually. The precise form it will take may vary, even among people who appear to speak alike, since each mind develops, in response to individual experiences, in part independently. I, the author, have my 'English', as a system I acquired as I grew up in my own family. You, the reader, may have similarly acquired your own 'English'. Our individual 'Englishes' are at least sufficiently alike for you to understand, or feel you understand, what I am writing. Only they, however, are real. Any 'English' in a wider sense will be a secondary abstraction.

Yet it is this secondary construct that most interests us. We all talk in practice, once more, of such languages as English, Arabic, or French; of Egyptian Arabic or the Arabic of Cairo, of American or Irish English, and so on. Their identity, however, is an interesting philosophical problem, and it is in the nature of philosophy that we will often find revealing problems and obscurities in what seems the commonest of common sense.

Chapter 7
How much is systematic?

To say that languages are systems is in principle to draw a line around what we are studying. 'Everything that forms a system is linguistics; what is not a system isn't language.' A line drawn in another way might nevertheless include much that is far less obviously determinate.

How many different ways, for instance, can the voice move up or down in saying *No*? Suppose one says it firmly to a child, who is about to do what they should not do. The pitch, in that case, might start in the mid to low part of a speaker's range, and move slightly lower. What if it instead begins much higher, and then falls more sharply from there? That might possibly be said in protest: 'no, I am not going to do what you want'. Now start in the mid range; let the pitch at first fall slightly, but then raise it higher. This might perhaps express doubt as to what has just been said: 'is that really not so?'. Then let the fall again start higher, with the rise too higher in turn: that might merely intensify a feeling of surprise. Such patterns vary from one form of English to another. There will be readers, therefore, whose impressions may not match what I have said. Like other features, they too can change. Older British speakers, for example, often comment on the way the pitch now tends to rise, in speakers in their teens or twenties, at the end of statements.

Are differences in pitch, however, like those between singular and plural, or between contrasting patterns of word order? We can clearly try to see them in that way. Thus, in one analysis, a relatively high pitch contrasts with a relatively low; one that is 'extra high', as a further parameter, with one 'not extra high'. How far, though, can an analysis like that be taken? Thus, to continue, *No!* could at the outset have a middish pitch but be cut short: this is sometimes what is represented, partly, by the spelling *Nope!* It could alternatively be prolonged to varying degrees, with or without slight variations in pitch. How far, moreover, is it possible to pin down differences in meaning, among 'firmness', 'doubt', 'surprise', and so on?

In one sense, this is clearly part of 'language', and of a specific language as specific people speak it. Yet, if differences in pitch or meaning cannot be reduced to exact contrasts, they are strictly not part of one's knowledge of it as a system. Some linguists have described them as peripheral to 'language', or as having no part in it. They are features of speech, even 'regular' in an everyday sense; but indeterminate.

Can patterns that affect words also be less systematic? A rule can have 'exceptions': thus the rule in English for a regular plural has exceptions, such as *mice* from *mouse*, or *women* (['wɪmɪn]) from *woman* (['wʊmən]). What, though, of the rules abstracted from relations between words or larger units? Do these have exceptions, or are they possibly more slippery?

Rules as constraints

One fascinating illustration is the use of words in -*self* or -*selves*: her**self**, for example, or them**selves**. Take, for example, *Mary got herself paid*. In *Mary got her paid*, where there is no -*self*, *her* and *Mary* will refer to different people, someone who is paid and someone else called 'Mary'. But *herself* would not refer to someone else. Compare *The boys got **themselves** paid*, in contrast with *The boys got **them** paid*. *The boys* and *them* could only refer to different individuals; *the boys* and *themselves* cannot.

The form in -*self* or -*selves* is thus linked, as grammars put it, to an 'antecedent': *herself* to the antecedent *Mary*; *themselves* to the antecedent *the boys*. One prospective rule prescribes, then, that a word in -*self* or -*selves* must take its reference from an expression earlier in a sentence with whose meaning it is compatible. If the rule is watertight, such words will always be used in that way.

This rule has been intensely studied, and, on closer analysis, it breaks down into three parts. Each is effectively a constraint on what, hypothetically, will make sense in the language. If the hypothesis is right, then break the bounds of any of them and what one says will be at least odd.

The first constraint is simply that a form in -*self* or -*selves* must have an antecedent. It should thus make sense to say to someone *Get **her** paid!*, since *her* has no -*self*; but not *Get **herself** paid!*, where there is no earlier expression to which *herself* is linked. The rule we have identified is, in part, confirmed if no examples like this last one can be found.

The second constraint is that antecedents have to be compatible in meaning. *Herself* is both singular and feminine; thus in *Mary got herself paid* it will be compatible with *Mary*, as the name of an individual girl or woman. It is hard, however, to make sense of *The boys got herself paid*, if *the boys* refers, as it usually does, to two or more individuals who are male.

The third constraint is that the antecedent is within a sentence. The facts, however, are in this case not so simple. Take, for example, *Mary said Jane got herself paid*. *Mary* and *Jane* are both names compatible with *herself*; therefore, from what has been said so far, we might expect its antecedent to be either. Instead, however, it seems clear that payment would be to Jane. Otherwise the natural form would be not *herself* but *her*. The reason many have suggested is that there are smaller units, within sentences, by which links to antecedents are still further constrained. We can mark their

14. Noam Chomsky (1928–).

boundaries with brackets, and, in this case, *Jane* and *herself* are
within one: *Mary said* [***Jane** got **herself** paid*]. Therefore they are
linked. *Mary*, however, is outside it: ***Mary** said* [*Jane got **herself**
paid*]. Therefore, if the hypothesis is right, that link is excluded.

This third kind of constraint has played a large role in the case Noam
Chomsky (see box) has presented for a 'Universal Grammar'. What

Noam Chomsky

The direct influence of Saussure (see box in the last chapter) was increasingly replaced by that of Chomsky (Fig. 14) from the 1960s onwards. His first book, *Syntactic Structures* (1957), was already famous for his concept of a 'generative grammar', as a set of rules for what is 'grammatical' in a language; also for a 'transformational grammar', as one kind of grammar in that sense.

His most important idea, however, is that basic properties of language are determined by our genes. In investigating a specific language, we abstract the structures in the minds of speakers that must have developed, early in their childhood, as they came to master it. But we must then explain how that development was possible. The more intricate such structures are, the less likely it appears that they develop solely on the basis of the speech that children hear, with the contexts in which it is heard and other relevant external 'input'. If we cannot explain them in that way, the only alternative is that they are genetically inherited.

To say that someone 'knows' a language is in his account to say that (at least among other things) they know its grammar. Hence, to use Chomsky's term, what every human being must inherit is a 'Universal Grammar' (abbreviated 'UG'). His conception of UG is still constantly evolving; but in an influential theory he developed in the 1980s, it included principles of grammar that would hold for every language, with 'parameters', whose alternative values were fixed differently in languages of different types, as the minds of children developed their knowledge of them.

> **Convincing or not, the argument is one that many people far beyond linguistics have found very challenging.**

holds for forms like *her* and *herself* will hold similarly, at least, for other elements: especially, at a very abstract level, in the way a unit like those in square brackets is defined. What holds for English also holds, in part at least, for other languages. The theory, therefore, is that the constraints in English realize, in a way in part specific to this language, still more abstract principles that apply to languages in general. The way they operate is through genetic inheritance.

Are rules absolute?

It is tempting to stop at this point. Many textbooks do, and what follows is a sample of the detail left aside. Our question, however, was whether systems of rules were wholly determinate. How faithfully does actual speech or writing follow them?

Take, for a start, the exception illustrated in the box opposite. In both examples forms in -*self* are used without an antecedent, directly contravening the first part of our rule. In both, again, the speaker could have used a form without -*self*: *I and most other GPs*; *either **hím** or* (with parallel emphasis) *some **óther** minister*. In both, however, forms in -*self* are joined to another expression: in one, by *and*, to *most other GPs*; in the other as part of an '*either . . . or . . .*'. It is unlikely that, in the first example, *myself* would have been used on its own: *the guidelines that myself adhere to*. Instances with *and*, however, are in no way strange in educated British English. It would be odd, for example, to get a message saying *Myself cannot come this afternoon*; but one beginning *Pat and myself . . .*, or *Our wives and ourselves . . .*, would in practice be quite normal. In the second of these, *our wives and we* might be, if anything, less likely.

It is possible that, at this point, we are dealing with no more than an exception. In general, forms in -*self* require an antecedent; but not, specifically, when they are joined to parallel expressions in this way. There are other cases, however, where an independent factor seems to intervene.

Why not forms without -*self*?

the guidelines that myself and most other GPs adhere to
(member of General Medical Council, radio interview, March 1999)

Would it be possible at some stage to require either himself or some other minister to . . .
(question in House of Commons, December 1992)

Let us return, for example, to the basic contrast between forms in -*self* and forms without -*self*. In *He extricated himself*, the 'himself' (if we can put it that way) is again identical to the 'he'; in *He extricated him*, the 'him' in contrast must be someone different. What then of *myself* and *me*? At first sight, these too seem to fit the pattern perfectly. In *I extricated myself*, the form in -*self* is again linked to an antecedent. The person referred to would be the same 'I', who is the speaker. There is then an apparent contradiction in *I extricated me*. *Me* has no -*self*, and the person it refers to should accordingly be different. How can that be, however, when it too refers to the speaker? By this logic, *me* makes no sense.

Following the same logic, one would usually say *You extricated yourself*; not *You extricated you*. What people usually say is not necessarily, however, what they always say, in all circumstances. Look, for example, at the three examples in the box overleaf. In the first, the form could equally have been *for yourself*. Note, however, that *you* will be read with emphasis: *You do an MBA for **yóu***. In the next, *me* could alternatively have been *myself*. Again, however, it is emphasized: *I bought it for **mé***. The speaker was distinguished from the rest of the family, dog included. In the third example, *me* and *I* both have a similar prominence: *Í'd have held the gun at **mé***. Here, too, the script could have read *myself*. One might speculate, however, that the actual 'me', at whom the gun would have been held, is subtly different from an imaginary 'I' who would be in the other character's shoes.

In the light of these examples, could one after all say something like ***Yóu** extricated **yóu***? It is hard to imagine circumstances in which one might. It is not easy, however, when we are dealing with a factor such as emphasis, to draw a line between what is possible and what is not.

Why is there no *-self*?

You do an MBA for you: it's the first step to being an entrepreneur.

(advertisement in *The Economist*, 1990s)

I bought the [make of car] for me, but everyone else thinks it's theirs.

(advertisement on TV, 2002)

If I'd heard what you'd heard I'd have held a gun at me.
(film, date untraced)

Now look, finally, at our last box. The rule as we described it would exclude, for instance, *Mary said* [*they got herself paid*]: on the one hand, *herself* could not have *they* as an antecedent, since their

94

meanings are incompatible; on the other, it could not be linked to *Mary*, which is outside the unit in square brackets. Yet the sentence from Trollope is exactly like this: ***She*** (the antecedent) *was sure* [*that he* (incompatible) *would never fall in love with **herself***]. Both this and the example from Jane Austen override the rule that we have given; and, although both are from novels written in the 19th century, neither is at all unclear to readers in the 21st. In Jane Austen's case, the brackets would be, similarly: [*that Mr Knightley must marry no one but herself*]. It is very hard, however, to see what else she could have written. *No one but her* would have made sense, but not so obviously the one intended. The character 'Emma' is the 'her' of *through her*, and, if *no one but her* was read without emphasis on *her*, it could easily be taken to refer to someone else (Harriet in the context). At best it might once more refer to either of them: compare, in a more straightforward illustration, *Mary said* [*that he had paid her*].

Where is the antedecedent?

She was sure that he would never fall in love with herself.
(Trollope, *Ayala's Angel*, 23)

It darted through her, with the speed of an arrow, that Mr Knightley must marry no one but herself.
(Jane Austen, *Emma*, III.11)

Bagshaw was at once attentive to the idea of an American biographer of X. Trapnel seeking an interview with himself.
(Anthony Powell, *Temporary Kings*, 4)

For the structure of the last example in the box, compare *Mary liked* [*Jane paying it to herself*]. *Herself*, especially if not emphasized, will again be linked, within the brackets, to *Jane*. Now in the passage from Powell, *himself* is compatible, in similar brackets, with *an American biographer of X. Trapnel*. Yet that is not its antecedent. Instead it has to be understood with *Bagshaw*, which is again outside this unit. Why, in that case, did Powell not write *him*? One reason, perhaps, is that it might be taken to refer to Trapnel, even though by this stage in the story he is dead.

Where do such illustrations leave us?

There is nothing here to suggest that linguists should not try to formulate rules. The principles that Chomsky and his followers have identified do tell us a great deal about these forms in English at least. They are nevertheless abstractions, and abstractions can be on many different levels.

At the highest level, many linguists search for constraints that reveal the character of language, or of languages, in general. That is the excitement, above all, of Chomsky's Universal Grammar. If he is right, it is entirely reasonable to concentrate on what belongs to it, and abstract away from interfering factors that do not.

At a lower level of abstraction, there are what we might call rules for exceptions. They run counter to more general principles, but their scope could still be precise. Perhaps, for instance, there are exact conditions under which one might say something like *myself and most other GPs*. At a still lower level, explanations may be harder to pin down. In particular, we must often pay attention to the very specific circumstances in which people are speaking or writing on specific occasions.

The way such words are used can also shade into the detail that belongs more readily to a dictionary. Compare, for example, *They controlled themselves* with *They behaved themselves*. In the first, *themselves* contrasts with *them*, and could easily be emphasized:

*They controlled them**sélves*** (but not, in contrast, others). In the other, we are dealing with a single complex unit ('to behave oneself'). The form in *-self* is part and parcel of it; and, in contrast, *They behaved **them*** does not readily make sense. Forms like this might also be found in a dictionary of idioms. Take, for example, *You must pull yourself together*. 'To pull oneself together' has a meaning as a whole, which does not precisely follow from the literal meanings of these words. Could one extend this to, for instance, *You must pull him together*? Eventually we will find that we are struggling to set limits to word play.

One of the beauties of language is that it can be investigated at such varied levels of abstraction. Many linguists find the details an unending marvel, and some positively relish its less systematic aspects, which most clearly reflect the passing circumstances in which people speak or write. For many others, the most abstract patterns are profoundly revealing, and to get at them all else is set aside. Linguistics has to be a broad church, with a place for minds of either bent.

Chapter 8
Sounds

As words and meanings contrast, so do units of sound. A [d] in English, in words such as *den* or *door*, is in itself distinct from [t], in *ten* or *tore*, or [p] in *pen* or *pour*. The [ɛ] of *ten* can be abstracted as another unit, in contrast with the [a] of *tan* or [ɪ] in *tin*. Stress on the first syllable, in ['bɪləʊ] (*billow*), is similarly in contrast with stress on the second syllable, in [bɪ'ləʊ] (*below*). The basic evidence is, naturally, that the words as wholes have different meanings.

In their sounds, too, different languages have different systems. In Spanish, for example, there are five distinct vowels. They fit, conveniently, the letters of the Roman alphabet: *a* in, for example, *caro* 'dear' or *carne* 'meat'; *e* in *dedo* 'finger' or *dentro* 'inside'; and so on. Think, however, of the problem Spanish speakers face in trying to learn English. English does not just have many more vowels, but different kinds of vowel follow, in part, different rules.

That there are more of them is obvious at once. The [ɛ] of *dead*, for instance, has a sound like that of Spanish *e* in *dedo* or *dentro*; so, too, however, has the [eɪ] of English *dado* (['deɪdəʊ]) and, in many accents, a long [ɛː], or diphthong [ɛə], in *dared*. The different rules may be less obvious. There are many words, however, ending in vowels such as [eɪ] or [iː]: *day* ([deɪ]), *tea* ([tiː]). There are also words like *paying* or *seeing* in which [eɪ] or [iː] combines with a

Two classes of vowels in English

The transcription we are using is specifically of English in the south of Britain: in other forms the contrasts can be different. In this form, however, one class has six members, all of which can be distinguished in words of one syllable, with a consonant following.

Class A ('short')

ɪ	(*pit*)	ʊ	(*put*)
ɛ	(*pet*)	ɒ	(*pot*)
a	(*pat*)	ʌ	(*putt*)

All six can also be distinguished in stressed syllables in general: thus, in the first column, *bitter* (['bɪtə]), *better* (['bɛtə]), *batter* (['batə]). Again, however, all six are distinguished only if a consonant follows.

Class B also has six members, two transcribed as 'long' and the other four as 'diphthongs'.

Class B

iː	(*beat*)	uː	(*boot*)
eɪ	(*bait*)	əʊ	(*boat*)
ʌɪ	(*bite*)	aʊ	(*bout*)

These do contrast without a following consonant: thus, in the first column, *pea* ([piː]), *pay* ([peɪ]), *pie* ([pʌɪ]).

The arrangement in columns reflects, in particular, the nature of the diphthongs in Class B. In [eɪ] and [ʌɪ], the change in sound is towards that of the [ɪ] of *pit*; in [əʊ] and [aʊ], it is towards that of the [ʊ] in *put*.

vowel directly following. With an [ε] or [ɪ] such patterns are excluded: we find no contrasts, for example, between forms like [deɪ] and [dɛ] or [tiː] and [tɪ]. This is characteristic of a class of vowels conventionally called 'short' (Class A in the box). We can thus abstract a general rule by which this kind of vowel is possible only under certain conditions.

The units that such rules refer to are themselves abstractions. How do they relate, then, to the physical reality of the sound that comes from speakers' mouths?

The answer might, at first, seem very simple. In writing, say, *pat* one first writes the letter *p*, then the letter *a*, and then the letter *t*. It is therefore very easy to assume that, when the same word is 'pronounced', it can be divided into three successive 'sounds': first, a 'sound' [p]; then, as [p] ends, a second 'sound' [a]; then, as that ends in turn, a final 'sound' [t]. Each 'sound' would thus form a distinct 'slice' of the total signal that a speaker transmits. When words themselves are combined, they in turn form larger 'slices'.

If matters were so simple I would not, of course, put terms like 'sound' or 'slice' in scare quotes. Look, however, at the spectrogram in Fig. 15. The same recording was used earlier, in Chapter 1, to confirm that signals like this were continuous. At that point all we needed was a wave form (Fig. 1). The spectrogram is more informative, but 'slices' corresponding to words still cannot be seen. Nor is it always obvious where 'sounds' corresponding to a vowel or consonant begin or end.

To see why, we must understand the basic mechanisms by which the acoustic signal is produced.

How sounds are made

Take, for example, the sound 'Ah', as said aloud to a doctor who wants to examine a patient's throat. This is one of the simplest

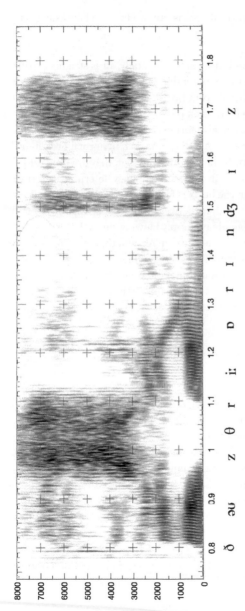

15. Spectrogram of *those three oranges*. A spectrogram displays the changing levels of acoustic energy across a range of frequencies. The time scale, measured arbitrarily in tenths of a second, is from left to right, the scale of frequencies, in Hertz (Hz), is from bottom to top. Higher levels of energy, above a set threshold, are registered by darker traces. The accompanying transcription indicates approximately when successive vowels and consonants are heard: IPA [ðəʊz] (*those*) [θriː] (*three*) [ɒrɪndʒəz] (*oranges*).

sounds the human vocal organs can produce. So how exactly is it done?

As one says this, and in speaking generally, air is steadily expelled from the lungs. If in doubt on that point, try saying 'Ah' for several seconds, and eventually your breath will run out. At the base of the throat this stream of air then passes through the larynx, which is a box-like organ with a valve formed by two parallel folds of membrane. These are the vocal cords and, in normal breathing, they are held apart. In saying 'Ah', however, they are brought together, so that they vibrate, at a frequency determined by their tension, as air from the lungs is forced between them. This vibration makes the difference, then, between a sound like that of 'Ah' and one that might be made by simply blowing through the mouth. It also makes the difference between 'Ah' and the sound of 'h' in, for example, 'Ha'. In saying 'Ha', a stream of air is audibly expelled; but at the beginning, for a fraction of a second, the vocal cords are not yet vibrating. Their vibration also makes the difference between 'Ah' said at a higher pitch, where it is faster, or at a lower pitch, where it is slower.

The stream of air then passes into the throat and mouth, which act as a complex resonator. As the vocal cords vibrate, so too does the column of air within it; and, by varying the size and shape of the space in which it is enclosed, one causes it to resonate selectively across a range of frequencies. In saying 'Ah', the gap between the jaws is widened and the tongue is flattened and retracted. One can see this, naturally, if one takes the doctor's view by looking in a mirror. But now compare a sound that might be written 'Eee'. The gap between the jaws is narrowed and, if 'Eee' is exaggerated, it is likely that the lips will be stretched sideways. Behind them, the body of the tongue has also been pushed to the front. Since the size and shape of the chamber has changed, so has its resonance. Sounds like 'Ah' and 'Eee' are distinguished, in particular, by three varying concentrations of acoustic energy below a frequency of 3,000 Hz. In the case of 'Ah', two are at lower frequencies, and the third higher. In the case of 'Eee', one is near the top of this range of frequencies, another a little lower, one a lot lower.

Similar concentrations show up as the horizontal bands in Fig. 15: compare, in particular, their frequencies above the points at which the [iː] of *three* and [ɒ] of *oranges* are placed in the transcription. It will at once be obvious, however, why the [iː] and [ɒ] cannot form two precisely separated 'slices'. As one says this, one can see in a mirror that the tongue is quickly drawn back. In front the lips are also moving, and that too modifies the resonator. Such changes are continuous, and as they take place the acoustic signal will continuously vary. This variation shows up in the way the bands in Fig. 15 bend across the range of frequencies.

In speech in general, sound effects like these combine with several others, some of which can also be sensed separately. Say 'Shh', for example, as you might in telling someone to keep quiet. Little can be seen, in this case, in a mirror. One can feel, however, that the tongue is raised towards the front of the mouth, and that its sides are in firm contact with the sockets of the upper side teeth. Air flowing from the lungs is thus forced through a narrowed passage in the middle, towards the front teeth that lie in its path. We can think of this passage as like a gorge through which a river passes, and the teeth as like a row of boulders. The flow of water, when it hits them, is already fast and turbulent. The air stream is affected similarly, and the sound of 'Shh' is the sound of its turbulence.

In saying 'Shh', the valve formed by the vocal cords is open; in saying 'Ah', they are again vibrating. In a word, then, like *Shah* it is easy to identify a consonant ([ʃ]) and vowel ([ɑː]) with 'sounds' whose character and timing are distinct. The [θ] of *three* is also characterized by turbulence, produced in this case with the tip of the tongue placed so that air is forced through the top teeth. The acoustic effect, as can be seen in Fig. 15, is again very different from the 'Eee'-like character of the vowel.

It is not nearly so easy, however, to make out an [r] between [θ] and [i:]. An [r] in, for example, [ri:d] (*reed*) is also produced with the vocal cords vibrating. It is obvious, however, that they are controlled by muscles separate from the tongue and those controlling the position of the lower jaw and other relevant organs. Therefore their actions can be coordinated in much subtler ways.

Stops

Let us return, for a clearer illustration, to *pat* [pat]. It can be felt at once, and seen in a mirror, that as this word begins the lips are briefly pressed together. They are also pressed together in *mat* [mat], with air passing through the nose. The passage through the nose then acts briefly as a further resonator. But in [pat] that passage too is closed off, as it also was, by implication, in both 'Ah' or 'Shh'. Thus, for an instant, air cannot pass out anywhere.

Consonants in which an air flow is blocked are described as 'stops'. It seems, then, that in [pat] we might distinguish, as three 'slices', first a stop [p]; then [a]; then a final stop [t]. In the case of [t] the blockage cannot be seen in a mirror; one can feel, however, that the tip of the tongue is brought briefly into contact with an area behind the front teeth. That too closes off an outward flow of air; pressure behind this closure rises; and the sound heard at the end is that of air escaping as this second blockage is released.

The 'sound' of [a] would thus lie in between two periods of closure. 'Sound', though, is still in inverted commas, and it will already be clear that matters cannot be quite so straightforward.

Consider first the movements of the organs above the larynx. It is obvious that as the lips are closed, the gap between the jaws is also narrowed. That must be so, accordingly, in the production, as we represent it, of [p]. As the lips are opened, the lower jaw is then swung downwards, carrying with it the front part of the tongue, which is already flattened in the mouth. That is the transition, as we describe it, between [p] and [a]. In the transition between [a] and [t], the lower jaw swings upwards once more; and, as this happens, the tongue is raised, in part independently, towards a target position for that consonant. Between the [p] and [t] the size and shape of the resonator are continuously changing. Therefore the acoustic signal also changes continuously, in the kind of way already seen, in Fig. 15, in the transition between [iː] and [ɒ].

A famous experiment in the 1950s showed just how important such transitions are. In saying *tap* or *cat* instead, the movements of the lips, the tongue, and lower jaw are different; so, in spectrograms, the bands representing concentrations of acoustic energy will bend differently. The method, therefore, was to synthesize speech artificially from the input of such bands alone. Subjects could still perceive the difference between consonants like [p] and [t] and [k], even though the only other things they heard were periods of silence.

So what, next, makes the difference between [p] and [b] or [t] and [d]? For each pair of consonants the movements of the lips or tongue are similar. The crucial differences lie in the times at which the vocal cords are open or vibrating.

Differences like those in Fig. 16 (overleaf) are typical of many English speakers. In both words the passage through the mouth is closed twice, and in each case a vowel follows. Look then, in particular, at the points at which these periods of closure end. In *totter*, the vocal cords do not begin to vibrate immediately. There is therefore an interval in which air continues to flow freely through them; and, as the blockage is removed, the flow measured at the lips will be still higher. In *dodder*, however, the vocal cords begin to vibrate immediately. There is no interval and, as the blockage is reduced, the air flow will be lower. A similar difference would be registered in pairs of words like *poppy* and *Bobby*. A [b] is produced, before vowels, when the vocal cords begin to vibrate as the blockage ends; a [p] when their vibration is significantly delayed.

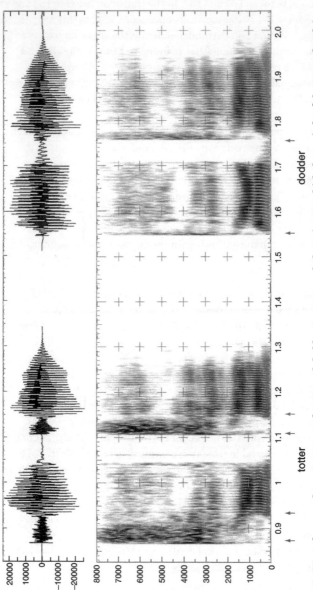

16. Wave forms and spectrograms of *totter* and *dodder*. Arrows mark the points at which the periods of closure end and, in *totter*, the intervals before the vocal cords begin to vibrate.

Some other differences can be registered. When [d] is produced between vowels, as in *dodder*, the vocal cords will be vibrating earlier, and this vibration tends to die out (as can just be seen in Fig. 16) after the passage of air through the mouth is blocked off. In the case of [t], it stops immediately. A vowel before [d] also tends (as again in Fig. 16) to be longer. Such differences, however, are again in the transitions between vowels and stops, not in steady state distinctions within stops as such.

Fig. 16 illustrates the differences as made by many English speakers: not, be warned, all. For it is obvious that there are other possibilities, and they are widely registered in other languages.

Some languages have no contrasts like these: they include in general those indigenous to Australia. The same consonant will accordingly be realized in ways that may sound, to a speaker of European languages, as at times more '[p]-like' or more '[t]-like' and at other times more '[b]-like' or more '[d]-like'. There are further differences, however, within Europe itself. An English speaker who sets out to learn Italian, for example, may not be quite aware of what is involved. Typically, however, in a word like *babbo* 'daddy', the vocal cords begin to vibrate while the lips are still closed for the initial consonant, and continue to vibrate through both the vowels that follow and the second closure. In a word like *pappa* '(bread) pap', they begin to vibrate at the point at which the initial closure ends and cease vibrating for a period coinciding with the second closure. In other languages there are three-way contrasts of this kind. In one set of stops, the point at which the vocal cords begin to vibrate is significantly later than the ending of the closure, as typically for [t] in English; such consonants are conventionally described as 'aspirated'. In another set, the timing is like that of the 'p' in Italian: no vibration during the closure, but no significant delay when it ends. In another set, the timings are more 'b-like'. This distinguishes three of four different sets of stops in, for example, Urdu and Hindi.

Beyond vowels and consonants

A word like *pat*, then, is not physically three 'slices' of sound,
[p] + [a] + [t]. Units like [p], [a], and [t] are instead abstractions,
valid within a system. It is worth asking, therefore, whether all
appropriate abstractions are like those that alphabetic writing
represents.

Let us look, for example, at the roles played by the lips. When one
says 'Ah', with the jaw wide open, they too are stretched open and
the postures they can assume are limited. It is obvious, however,
that although they are part of a wider assembly, they are also in part
independent. In saying 'Ooo', the lips are pursed or rounded; but it
is possible to hold all else constant and, while doing so, to stretch
them sideways. That is the posture they will also tend to have in
saying 'Eee'. In 'Ooo' and 'Eee' the tongue too has a different
posture; but again one can say 'Eee' and, holding the tongue
constant, round the lips instead. This is one way, for example, in
which English speakers learning French are taught the vowel in
words like *lune* 'moon' (IPA [lyn]).

It is therefore possible to see 'lip-rounding', in a word like French
lune, as itself one kind of abstract unit. But such a unit will
potentially cut across the vowels and consonants of an alphabet, the
IPA included.

Take, for example, a word in English like *clue*. The initial
consonants, in the usual IPA transcription, are identical to those of,
for example, *clean*. The vowels which follow are then defined, in
part, by postures of the lips like those of 'Ooo' and 'Eee': [kluː]
(*clue*), where they are 'rounded', as opposed to [kliːn] (*clean*). There
is no reason, however, why the timing of lip postures should match
those of the tongue especially. In *two clues*, for example, *two* ends
with the same vowel, and in saying this the lips are likely to be
rounded throughout all or most of both words. Compare the same
[kl], as it is represented in this alphabetic format, in *three cleans*. In

three clues, the posture of the lips is likely to change rapidly as soon as the [iː] of *three* ends; similarly, but in the opposite way, in *two cleans*. If *clues* is said on its own, their posture may again be similar throughout. Is it right, then, to imply that rounding is a characteristic of the [uː] alone?

Such questions arise seriously in languages such as Turkish. The box overleaf illustrates a regular pattern in which a rounded or 'unrounded' posture of the lips carries over from one syllable to the next. In a word like *köyün* 'of (a) village', the first vowel is similar to the 'ö' in German, with lip-rounding, and the second like the 'ü' in German, also with lip-rounding. In a word like *elin* 'of (a) hand', both vowels are instead 'unrounded', the lips tending to be spread. Each of these words has the ending of the genitive case ('of X'), which is one of many endings whose form varies in accordance with the syllable that precedes it. There is rounding in *köy* 'village', and there is rounding also in the *-ün* that follows. There is no rounding in *el* 'hand', and there is again no rounding in *-in*.

The pattern is described as one of 'vowel harmony', and the implication is that it is just the vowels that contrast. That is also implied by the way the words are written in the Turkish alphabet. This was first adopted in the 20th century, as part of a Westernizing programme pushed through, under Atatürk (Mustafa Kemal), in the years that followed the First World War. It distinguishes, exactly and efficiently, eight vowels: four (see box) which descriptions of the language class as rounded, four unrounded. Yet there is an alternative. In a word like *köyün* there is harmony, as we put it at the outset, between syllables. Nor, in reality, is the rounding characteristic merely of vowels. In this word the lips are in a pursed position from the beginning; they are pursed in the transition between syllables; and they are still pursed in the transition to 'n'. The 'harmony', in this light, is abstracted from both syllables as wholes.

The box also illustrates a second pattern, in which endings again

Regular patterns of 'vowel harmony' in Turkish

Examples are given of words with and without a genitive case ending (GEN). In the second and fourth columns, the syllable before the ending has a 'rounded' vowel: *ü* or *ö*, *u* or *o*. That of the ending (*-ün* or *-un*) is also rounded. In the first and third columns the corresponding vowel is 'unrounded': *i*, *e*, *ı*, or *a*. The 'GEN' ending (*-in* or *-ın*) is similarly unrounded.

In the first two columns, the vowel before the ending is described as 'front': front rounded *ü* or *ö*; front unrounded *i* and *e*. The ending too is also front: rounded *-ün* or unrounded *-in*. In the last two columns the vowels in question are instead 'back': back rounded *u* and *o*; back unrounded *ı* and *a*.

deniz	tütün	kadın	sabun
'sea'	'tobacco'	'woman'	'soap'
deniz-in	tütün-ün	kadın-ın	sabun-un
'sea-GEN'	'tobacco-GEN'	'woman-GEN'	'soap-GEN'
el	köy	adam	son
'hand'	'village'	'man'	'end'
el-in	köy-ün	adam-ın	son-un
'hand-GEN'	'village-GEN'	'man-GEN'	'end-GEN'

There are exceptions, but as regular patterns these affect many similar endings.

The vowels can then be classed as follows. In 'close' vowels the lower jaw and tongue are relatively higher, in 'open' vowels relatively lower.

	Front		Back	
	Unrounded	**Rounded**	**Unrounded**	**Rounded**
Close	i	ü	ı	u
Close	e	ö	a	o

'harmonize'. In a word like *sonun* 'of (an) end', *son* 'end' and *-un* 'GEN' are both rounded; but the postures of the tongue, especially, distinguish them from *ö* and *ü*. In *adamın* 'of (a) man', both *adam* and *-ın* (note there is no dot in the writing) are instead unrounded, but these too are distinct from *e* and *i* in *elin*. To produce the sound of 'ı' the best advice, for speakers of English, is to say a word like *push* while trying to spread the lips sideways. The posture of the lips is then like that of 'i', but that of the tongue is different.

The tongue is naturally a much more complex organ, and the postures it assumes, with those of the lower jaw, affect the shape and volume of the resonator along its whole length, from the larynx to the teeth and lips. The way these vowels are classified must thus involve a further process of abstraction. It is clear, however, that they form pairs. As *i* is to *ü*, so *ı* is to *u*: the evidence for that is in the way the 'GEN' and other endings vary. As *e* is to *ö* so, correspondingly, *a* is to *o*. If we then compare, say, *ö* and *o* one salient difference is that, in the case of *ö*, the body of the tongue is relatively towards the front of the mouth, whereas, in *o*, it is relatively towards the back. The same holds, individually, for other pairs distinguished on the same dimension: *i* versus *ı*; *ü* versus *u*; also (do not think of vowels spelled this way in English) *e* versus *a*.

Again, however, the effect is not just in one 'slice' of a syllable. The 'k', for instance, of *köy* 'village' is not the same, in terms of the precise posture of the tongue, as that of *kadın* 'woman'. Nor, for comparison, is the '[k]' of English *key* ([ki:]) objectively the same as that of *car* ([ka:]), though we transcribe them similarly. In the case

Sounds

of Turkish we could argue once more that the 'harmony' is abstracted from successive syllables as wholes.

Not all linguists will agree. We must always remember, however, that in talking of 'sound' units we are dealing with abstractions. Their relation to the physical reality of speech can be fascinatingly complex.

Chapter 9
Language and the brain

Our species, *Homo sapiens*, has a remarkably large brain. What is remarkable is not its absolute size: a largish animal can be expected in any case to have a bigger brain than, say, a mouse or a cat. What matters is the relation between the size and structure of the brain and the overall size of the body. By one measure, we are five times 'brainier', in a physical sense, than the trend in placental mammals generally.

Our nearest relatives also have a relatively large brain. So too, on the evidence of fossils from 3 million years BP, did the animals traditionally classed as 'hominid' or 'man-like'. Within a million years, however, *H. habilis* was already 'brainier' than any of them. This is the first species that palaeontologists assign to the same genus as ours. The skull of *H. erectus*, from around 1,000,000 BP, was still larger, and the trend continues until a period around 400,000 BP, when the earliest fossils have been assigned to our species. This 'braininess' we estimate from fossils is still purely physical. It is tempting, however, to associate its evolution not just with increased intelligence, but with specific patterns of behaviour that distinguish us from chimpanzees and other apes. Speech is one of the most striking; therefore many people have suggested that the origins of language, or at least of language-like forms of communication, lie in a period in which the brain became significantly larger.

This explosion in 'braininess', in man as in other primates, took place in the front especially of the cerebral cortex. The cortex is the part of the brain whose deeply folded surface lies immediately inside our head, and it is possible to deduce to some extent how it was folded in extinct species, by taking casts of the interior of fossil skulls. Some theories, therefore, have aimed for more detail. Let us assume, first, that control of language is located in specific areas of the cortex, and that we know where they are. Let us then assume that, if there is evidence of corresponding areas in a possible ancestor, they must have had a similar function. So, it is assumed, as they evolved so language-like behaviour evolved too.

This makes a lot of assumptions, the first of which is that we know if not how, then at least where language is controlled. How confident are we that we know this?

Why linguistics generally may not help

The 'how' especially is an awesome problem. We know how the sound of speech is generated, and how the vocal cords, the tongue, and other organs operate. We know how, in general, these and others organs are controlled by our nervous system. But we do not know how our brains determine the production of specific combinations of words. It is tempting to suppose that, since we analyse words into individual 'sounds', it too, for example when we say *no*, has to operate in terms of units such as [n] and [əʊ]. These do not even, however, exist literally in speech. They are abstractions established at a level of conscious understanding, by a process of analysis based in no way on brain functions. They may not offer any valid insight.

Take briefly, for comparison, the way we might suppose we see things. To see, for instance, that a car is whizzing past us is to perceive, in ordinary language, that its position is changing. We perceive it as a 'figure', in the term used by psychologists, moving relative to a 'ground', which is in turn formed by the perception of other things in view. It is therefore tempting to imagine that the patterns of light entering the eyes are analysed, in the brain, in something like that way. A figure would be identified from perceptions of shape and colour. The brain would at the same time register its movement from the way the patterns of light change. The perception of the car and of its movement would be inseparable aspects of a single experience.

At a conscious level this last statement is, of course, true. However, what brain scientists tell us is that a system dedicated to detecting movement is in reality distinct from ones detecting either shape or colour. The evidence has come largely from experiments on other animals whose eyes and brains have evolved similarly. The finding is confirmed, however, by rare instances in which a human brain is damaged, through disease or injury, so that one system only is disabled. In one case someone might see both the shape of the car and that it was moving, but have no perception of its colour. Red, blue, and so on would all look alike. There is also a well-studied case of someone who would see its shape and colour perfectly; but, bizarrely and disturbingly, not see that it was moving.

Such discoveries remind us that we are all outsiders when it comes to the grey matter in our heads. The systems linguists study are again abstractions from our conscious understanding of our minds and our behaviour. It would be naive to take these as a guide to how our brains must operate.

The warning applies not least to 'language' itself. What linguists study are, especially, the abstractions we describe as 'languages'. When we talk of 'language' in general, we are often talking, therefore, about properties of these. We must remind ourselves, however, of how much we then abstract away from. Speaking, for a start, is not the only form of meaningful behaviour. Without saying anything, people may point with their fingers, laugh or smile, put up their hands in despair, turn on their heels and walk away. In some societies, one bows to show respect; in others it would be ironic. All this is implicitly excluded as not 'language'. We also abstract away from many properties of speech itself. Speaking slowly, for example, can be meaningful; so can whispering, or shouting at the top of one's voice. That too, however, is not something linguists usually include. On this basis, many linguists ask how children come to master a specific language, in abstraction from their acquisition of all other forms of skill or knowledge. It seems reasonable to do so, in the light of conscious everyday experience. But it does not follow that the brains of children must develop correspondingly.

Take, for example, the way we talk about the meanings of words. 'Ways' would perhaps be better, since different linguists have different ideas of how they should be described. They tend to agree, however, that in saying what a word means we do not need to describe the world in general. A word like *fox*, say, has to be distinguished from contrasting words like *vixen*, *badger*, or *rabbit*. What is known, however, about the physiology or behaviour of foxes, or the numbers and distribution of particular species such as *Vulpes vulpes*, is not part of its meaning. In describing the meaning of *swim*, we have no reason to explain buoyancy or the mechanics of propulsion. This line can be hard to draw, and that perhaps might be a warning. Nevertheless it make sense to treat knowledge of how words are used as separate from what many linguists call 'encyclopaedic' knowledge.

Our brains, however, may be organized quite differently. Language is peculiar to our species: we 'have' it, and our nearest living relatives do not. But its evolution has been accompanied, to put it in the vaguest possible way, by a significant increase in intelligence. One obvious question is how intimately language and intelligence were linked. Language as we know it is a means of thought and not just of communication, and both language and intelligence in general are bound up with memory. It is not clear why we should assume that a 'linguistic memory', of how individual words are used in individual languages, has evolved separately.

Are there 'speech centres'?

The problem of 'where' language is controlled seems more amenable. Medical evidence, in particular, has long pointed to specific areas of the brain involved in understanding or producing speech. The problem, though, is that 'involved in' may mean strictly no more than it says.

The crucial areas for language are normally on the left side of the brain. The brain has a structure like the kernel of a walnut, with two similar-shaped 'hemispheres' linked physically towards the middle. The functions of the hemispheres are in many ways symmetrical. Each hemisphere controls limbs on the opposite side of the body, and receives input from the opposite half of our field of vision. These are functions, of course, we have in common with many other animals. In other ways, however, either hemisphere may be dominant: the right, for example, is dominant in one respect when people are left-handed. Where language is concerned it is the left that is dominant in all but a tiny minority of people. The evidence for this comes mainly from studies of people who have suffered brain damage. Tumours and cerebral strokes are sadly not rare; nor are injuries to the head in war, or in the unending accidents on our roads. A patient's speech is often affected in such circumstances, and when this happens the damage is almost always on the left side of the brain.

Two areas of the brain thought to be connected with language were named over a century ago (see box). If there do exist 'speech centres' in the brain, dedicated to the processing of language, these are by long tradition the main candidates. Many neurologists have since tried to be much more specific.

The evidence is in many ways quite puzzling. Take, for instance, a case history reported in the 1940s, from the University Clinic in Oslo. The patient ('Astrid L.') was a Norwegian woman whose brain had been injured badly on the left side, in an air raid in 1941. She

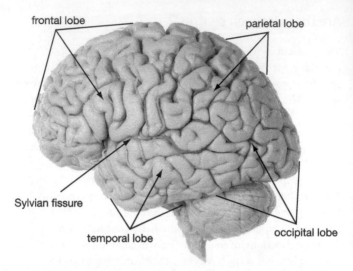

frontal lobe

parietal lobe

Sylvian fissure

temporal lobe

occipital lobe

Linguistics

17. **The left hemisphere of the human brain. The cortex is divided, in each hemisphere, into four lobes. The Sylvian fissure divides the frontal lobe from the temporal, immediately below 'Broca's area'.**

was at first unconscious, matter was spilling out, and X-rays revealed a large area of damage in the left frontal lobe. It is comforting, therefore, that this story has a happy ending. By the time the case was reported in 1947, she and her husband had had a baby, and she was in good health.

When she recovered consciousness in hospital, she was paralysed on her right side and at first not able to speak at all. Gradually, however, she got better, and two years later, on admission to the University Clinic, she could walk naturally and talk fluently. Her speech was marked, however, by a change above all in the 'melody of language'. The actual patterns varied but, in the words of the report, 'she never had the natural Norwegian accent when she had to link several words together in a sentence'. Thus, in particular, she often had a high pitch at the end of a sentence where one would expect it to be lowered, and in a specific sentence like *Jeg tok den* ('I took it')

'Broca's area' and 'Wernicke's area'

The first area is named after a 19th-century French physician, Paul Broca, who identified it in 1861 in a patient whose brain had suffered massive damage in this region, and, until death, was merely able to repeat what seemed a single syllable. The other is named after Carl Wernicke, who reported on two different cases in the 1870s. Both areas, looking from the side, are broadly central; both, looking from the top, lie on the outside. 'Broca's area' is more precisely in the frontal lobe, immediately above the deep fold called the Sylvian fissure. See Fig. 17 for these features. 'Wernicke's area' is located further back, roughly behind the temples. Brains differ in detail, and introductions give at best schematic diagrams. We should remember too that, in many patients, much more of the brain is actually affected.

Two classic patterns of disorder are in turn described as 'Broca's aphasia' and 'Wernicke's aphasia'. These are effectively labels for sets of apparent symptoms: on the one hand, lack of fluency and 'grammar'; on the other, fluency but lack of 'content'. But the implication is that different symptoms follow damage in different regions. Some investigators have suggested further that specific aspects of the apparent processing of language, like 'speech planning' (Broca's) and control of sentence structure (also Broca's), or 'speech comprehension' (Wernicke's), should be assigned to these areas. Support for this is often claimed from studies whose assumptions should be looked at critically, in which patients with brain damage have been presented, for example, with test sentences, written rather than spoken, and their responses in an experimental setting have been interpreted as evidence of how well they would be able to understand them, with reference to the grammatical structures, in particular, that linguists abstract.

she would overemphasize *den*. In normal speech, it would instead be reduced to form a single word-like unit with *tok*. Three years after the injury, she had to work hard at a test which required her to distinguish in pronunciation pairs of words (as there are in Norwegian) with contrasting changes in pitch. The result was that she seemed to other Norwegians to be speaking with a German accent. This was alas in the 1940s, when the Nazis had occupied Norway with no declaration of war, the Gestapo following, as usual, on the German army's heels. When 'Astrid L.' was first admitted to the University Clinic she complained bitterly, for example, that people were refusing to serve her in shops.

Why then were these aspects of her speech so noticeably not under control? The problem with its 'melody' did not lie in the control of pitch as such. 'Astrid L.' had been able to sing quite early in her convalescence, and when attending the clinic could sing perfectly in tune. It remains a mystery why, at this stage of her recovery, the pitch contours of speech were the main thing going wrong.

Many surveys deal with things observed to go wrong much more often. In the worst case, patients have effectively no speech at all, and show little sign of understanding what is said to them. That can also be an end result of a degenerative disorder such as Alzheimer's disease, which progressively destroys parts of the cortex in old age. In other cases people seem, at least, to understand speech normally: if asked, for instance, to do something they will do it as instructed. Their speech, however, may seem to be little more than one word, in the simple form we look up in a dictionary, followed by another. Suppose, say, such a patient is trying to tell you there are cats in the garden. You might hear a word you recognize as *cat*, but without a plural ending. After what may seem a false start or delay, you may hear another word recognizable as *grass*. But they would not be combined with forms like *are* or *the* in ways that make up a coherent sentence. Other patients can, in contrast, rattle away fluently. The problem, however, is precisely that they rattle, uttering streams of words to which we find it hard to attach a concrete meaning. There may also be more obvious evidence that the way they understand speech is impaired. Some patients may use nonsense words, like those in, for example, Lewis Carroll's 'Jabberwocky'. A sentence such as *And the mome raths outgrabe* (last line of 'Jabberwocky') can in part be understood quite easily. It is linked normally, by *and*, to the one before; *raths* may be plural, for example; the 'raths' referred to might, perhaps specifically, be in a state of 'momeness'. The point, however, of Carroll's poem, and analogously in this kind of speech disorder, lies in what on earth a rath that is mome might be. In less serious cases patients talk as if they had words on the tip of their tongue. If asked to pass a knife, say, they may do so; thus they know what *knife* means. Yet, to ask for one themselves, they may speak in a roundabout way: *Can I have? ... wait ... you know, you use it to cut things.*

Most theories of where language is controlled have been based on studying such patients. What we are reporting on, however, are effects not causes. In medical parlance, they can be classified at best as 'syndromes': that is, as collections of symptoms. AIDS, for comparison, was defined as a syndrome ('**A**cquired **I**mmune **D**eficiency **S**yndrome') in the light of symptoms first reported in the early 1980s; the hunt was then on to discover an agent that might cause it. The problem, in our case, is to explain abnormal patterns of behaviour in relation to brain damage in specific areas. But there are limits to how far this line of research can take us.

One obvious problem is that 'symptoms', as in other forms of broadly 'mental' disorder, are identified by our perceptions of how people behave normally. A patient might, for instance, make what we interpret as a grammatical error: *if Mary **come** tomorrow*, for example, not *comes*. Slips occur in normal speech too; but, when patients make them, they are liable to be seen as symptoms and clinicians have a label for them. What we notice, however, is inherently subjective. Take again, for example, the case of 'Astrid L.'. In recent surveys, her disorder is sometimes called a 'foreign

121

accent' syndrome, and said to be rare. This term, however, does not even describe speech as such, but how other members of a community, of whom the clinician is one, react to it. The original report, by G. H. Monrad-Kohn, coined instead the term 'dysprosody', referring to an abnormality in, for example, a pitch contour. It is hard to be sure that all 'dysprosodies' have been consistently recorded, when other abnormalities are present and a patient's speech is not so fluent that its 'foreignness' is all that strikes one.

Another warning is that language may be processed much more widely than appears from a specific injury. The reason why we talk of 'processing' is, in part, that patients can recover. It seems then that they must in some sense retain 'knowledge' of their language, both of words and of the rules by which they are combined, despite what might be diagnosed as a temporary problem in 'accessing' it, or making use of it when accessed. We are talking now, of course, in terms reflecting not just an insider's concept of a language, but a technical understanding of the kinds of information system we ourselves design. Let us at least imagine, however, that the brain works in that kind of way. Even so, the evidence of where damage is found could mislead us.

Think, for comparison, of how houses are lit up by electricity. The system might go wrong at one end if, say, a fuse blows and a room where people are sitting is plunged into darkness. That is easily remedied: if they are out of fuse wire, they can bring in leads from somewhere else. There might also be a problem, at the other end, in a power station that supplies the grid. Other stations, however, could compensate for it. Suppose, though, that a power line which supplies a whole town is brought down in a storm. The effect may then be devastating. The repair may take days, and meanwhile nothing that depends on the supply works. It does not follow, however, that since the line is down, and the power supply has gone dead, the place where electricity is generated must be where the storm struck.

The comparison with the brain is scarcely exact. Nevertheless we should be careful not to jump to conclusions about something we have not designed and do not understand. It could be that the damage we locate affects a 'pathway', as brain scientists describe it, in a system that is actually very diffuse.

What of the future?

This may all sound rather pessimistic. But hope springs eternal, and the future for the study of the brain in general does seem genuinely brighter.

One reason is that instruments get better and better. With brain scanners, it is now not only easier to locate exactly where brains have been damaged. It is also possible to observe where they are active as experiments are conducted. The most common technique is to infer activity in neurons from an increase in the flow of blood supplying energy to them. The brain needs energy, lots of it. We would need to eat far less if it was not so big. The method, therefore, is to measure indirectly how much is supplied to different areas. A higher blood flow is a sign that cells are working harder. Another technique, which seems still more promising, is to register activity of cells directly, by picking up minute electrical changes. The impact of brain scanning is, of course, much wider than in studying what happens when we speak. Linguistics is one discipline, however, that is poised to learn from what it might reveal.

It is important, however, that normal brains too should be studied. Patients, alas, are always with us and available for testing. An experiment, therefore, might be designed to study patterns of activity in subjects whose behaviour is abnormal in different ways, or whose brains have been affected in different regions. We must remember, though, that what we find may be in part due to the ways in which their brains are compensating for the damage.

Suppose, for the sake of comparison, that you lose the use of your right hand. There are things, then, that you used to do with two hands or with that hand alone, that you must now learn to do some other way. But you do learn. If you are right-handed, you will gradually force yourself to write, for example, with your left hand instead. That obviously involves your brain as well as your muscles, the more so as it is there that handedness is established. Now the processes of interest to linguists are within the brain itself. We cannot assume, however, that the way it works when it is damaged is the way it would work normally, minus, as it were, whatever used to go on in the parts affected. This might be rather like investigating, say, how people hold things by observing how they do it when one arm is amputated.

We can therefore expect more experiments in which brains of normal speakers are scanned. Another ground for hope, though, is perhaps more paradoxical. But the seeds of wisdom may lie in our realizing fully how mysterious the brain is.

There was a time when the brain was often seen as like a digital computer. At the 'hardware' level neurons are connected to other neurons, and electrical signals are simply passed along these circuits. That was, however, before neurologists knew as much about the chemistry of the brain as they know now and are still discovering. At a 'software' level, many investigators then believed that, if we could abstract a task that brains could be assumed to do, such as working out the grammatical structure of a sentence, and program a computer to do what we had abstracted, that would give us direct insight into how a system within the brain must deal with the input it receives. This is hopefully in the past, when computer science was itself more primitive. We had no reason, however, to assume that brains have dedicated 'software' systems, designed for sequences of subtasks into which some larger task, like understanding speech, is chopped up.

The truth is that we do not know how what is happening physically in the brain relates to an experience such as understanding a sentence. 'Understanding' is, of course, already strictly an abstraction from experience, though most linguists and psychologists scarcely question it. 'Sentences' are still more clearly an abstraction, though sufficiently valid at the level at which linguists usually work. There may, however, be a causal link more staggeringly complex than we yet conceive, between the physiological workings of the brain and the behaviour we observe and analyse, or the mental structures and impressions created by the interaction between them.

Further reading

Most general books on language and linguistics are textbooks aimed directly at undergraduate or postgraduate students. One that is not is David Crystal's *The Cambridge Encyclopaedia of Language*, 2nd. edn. (Cambridge University Press, 1997). There is also a good one-volume handbook, edited by Mark Aronoff and Janie Rees-Miller, *The Handbook of Linguistics* (Blackwell, 2000). Dictionaries of linguistics cover terminology especially: my own *Concise Oxford Dictionary of Linguistics* (Oxford University Press, 1997) is now available both in print and as part of *Oxford Reference Online*.

Linguistics is conventionally divided into several branches. Textbooks therefore tend to focus either on one branch specifically, or on branches seen as central. Two of the most successful general introductions are by Victoria Fromkin and Robert Rodman, *An Introduction to Language*, 6th edn. (Holt, Rinehart and Winston, 1998), and by Andrew Radford and others, *Linguistics: An Introduction* (Cambridge University Press, 1999). Another, longer text concentrates more narrowly on languages as systems of rules: Victoria Fromkin (ed.), *Linguistics: An Introduction to Linguistic Theory* (Blackwell, 2000).

The first separate branch, as many linguists see it, is phonetics: basically the study of how speech sounds are produced and perceived. For a leading introduction, by a distinguished researcher in this field, see Peter Ladefoged, *A Course in Phonetics*, 3rd edn. (Harcourt Brace,

1993). For the ways in which sounds are distinguished in different languages, see Peter Ladefoged and Ian Maddieson, *The Sounds of the World's Languages* (Blackwell, 1996).

Phonetics is distinguished from 'phonology', seen as the branch which deals with units of sound within a theory of languages as systems. For an introductory treatment see, for example, Philip Carr, *Phonology* (Macmillan, 1993). 'Morphology' is the branch which deals with grammatical contrasts within words: see, among others, my own introduction, *Morphology*, 2nd edn. (Cambridge University Press, 1991). 'Syntax' is the branch which deals with the relation between words and other units within sentences, and for many linguists is the most important. A student can usefully begin with Noël Burton-Roberts, *Analysing Sentences: An Introduction to English Syntax*, 2nd edn. (Longman, 1997); see too Rodney Huddleston, *English Grammar: An Outline* (Cambridge University Press, 1988), for a short account of English syntax and morphology in general. There are many introductions, at a technical level, to Chomsky's theory of syntax in particular: one both accessible and of moderate length is by Ian Roberts, *Comparative Syntax* (Arnold, 1997). For a presentation of Chomsky's life and work in general, by a prominent theoretician who has long been very sympathetic to his ideas, see Neil Smith, *Chomsky: Ideas and Ideals* (Cambridge University Press, 1999).

The study of meaning, in all aspects, is conventionally another branch, 'semantics'. Some textbooks actually treat semantics very narrowly: for a catholic account, by a distinguished scholar, see John Lyons, *Linguistic Semantics: An Introduction* (Cambridge University Press, 1995).

For many linguists other topics are peripheral, some very peripheral indeed. For the background to the origin of language, it is helpful to consult a general book on human evolution: see Steve Jones and others (eds.), *The Cambridge Encyclopaedia of Human Evolution* (Cambridge University Press, 1992). Two monographs on the diversification of language are both thought-provoking: Johanna Nichols, *Linguistic Diversity in Space and Time* (University of Chicago Press, 1992); Daniel

Nettles, *Linguistic Diversity* (Oxford University Press, 1999). So too is R. M. W. Dixon, *The Rise and Fall of Languages* (Cambridge University Press, 1997). Tore Janson, *Speak: A Short History of Languages* (Oxford University Press, 2002) is very readable.

For a popular introduction to how languages change, see Jean Aitchison, *Language Change: Progress or Decay?*, 3rd edn. (Cambridge University Press, 1991). For a general textbook in historical linguistics, by a leading specialist, see Lyle Campbell, *Historical Linguistics: An Introduction* (Edinburgh University Press, 1998); for a textbook introduction to the study of dialects, J. K. Chambers and Peter Trudgill, *Dialectology*, 2nd edn. (Cambridge University Press, 1998), from which I have adapted Map 1. Variation like that in New York is conventionally part of 'sociolinguistics': for a beginner's introduction see Janet Holmes, *An Introduction to Sociolinguistics*, 2nd edn. (Longman, 2002).

For the families of languages across the globe see, for example, the relevant articles in William Bright (ed.), *International Encyclopaedia of Linguistics*, 4 vols (Oxford University Press, 1992); a second edition, under a new editor, is in preparation. My dictionary of linguistics also has brief entries. The most recent survey of Indo-European in particular is by Robert Beekes, *Comparative Indo-European Linguistics: An Introduction* (John Benjamins, 1995). For a survey of different forms of writing, see T. Daniels and William Bright (eds.), *The World's Writing Systems* (Oxford University Press, 1996); for a relevant textbook, Florian Coulmas, *Writing Systems: An Introduction to their Linguistic Analysis* (Cambridge University Press, 2003).

For the human brain in general, see the popular introduction by Susan Greenfield, *Brain Story* (BBC, 2000), based on an excellent television series. For a recent introduction to the study of language in the brain, covering clinical evidence especially, see Loraine K. Obler and Kris Gjerlow, *Language and the Brain* (Cambridge University Press, 1999).

Index

Linguistics